Don't Miss Your Boat

Living Your Life with Purpose
in the Real World

Maryanna Young & Kim Fletcher

Don't Miss Your Boat
Living Your Life With Purpose in the Real World

By Maryanna Young and Kim Fletcher

Copyright © 2004

Published by:

Aloha Book Company
1312 North 19th Street
Boise, ID 83702
208 344 2733
alohabookcompany@aol.com
aloha@dontmissyourboat.com
www.dontmissyourboat.com

Cover and interior by NZ Graphics, www.nzgraphics.com

ISBN: 0-9762642-0-X

Library of Congress Control Number: 2004 097856

If you find typographical errors in this book we would love to know about them for further editions. Please email us at corrections@dont-missyourboat.com. They serve a purpose. Some people actually enjoy looking for them and we aim to please as many people as possible.

Copies of *Don't Miss Your Boat* are available at www.dontmissyour-boat.com, websites of the co-authors, retail locations throughout the US and Canada as well as at on line retailers including Amazon.com.

Quantity discounts are available.

Retail Price
$12.95 USA $19.95 Canada

Third Printing 2005

This book is dedicated to YOU, our reader.
It is our hope that you will find renewed excitement for
the journey of discovering and living your true purpose.

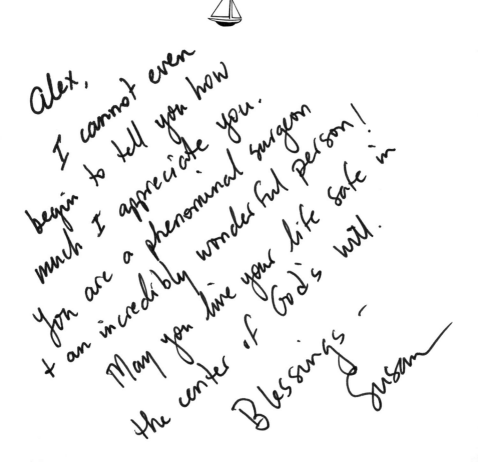

Alex,
I cannot even
begin to tell you how
much I appreciate you.
You are a phenomenal surgeon
+ an incredibly wonderful person!
May you live your life safe in
the center of God's will.

Blessings,
Susan

CONTENTS

ABOUT THE TITLE

Welcome to *Don't Miss Your Boat ... Living Your Life With Purpose in the Real World.* To begin, we thought you would enjoy knowing a bit about the origin of our title.

I have always loved boats ... all of them, whether a sleek red kayak or a grand sailing vessel. Offer me a ride and I will not *Miss the Boat.* In fact, I would likely cancel appointments or rearrange a day to make it to the dock on time. Once aboard, I am in my element ... the wind and the water can transform any day from ordinary to extraordinary. Somehow, the best of me emerges when I change into my deck shoes. I truly have a love affair with water and I willingly go wherever the current takes me. Ah, the adventure, surprise, and excitement associated with skimming over open water, whether it is a calm lake or a wave tossed sea. There is a sense of freedom that makes me want to refuse to disembark at the end of the journey!

'What on earth does this have to do with life purpose?' you might ask. Think about those individuals that seem to be living their best life ... life that is filled with purpose and passion. They wear their life as comfortably as I do my deck shoes. Like me onboard most any boat, they are most in their element doing what they are doing. They are living in passionate pursuit of a life that is worthy of abandoning other plans for one that leads to a feeling of great satisfaction and fulfillment. They find themselves willingly adhering to their chosen life even when it fails to be popular, exciting, and even when it takes them in unexpected directions. Simply put, they would not 'disembark' the unique life plan that bears their name ... they refuse to abandon their purpose because it is the place where priorities become clear, relationships grow deeper, and many days are invested in those people and things that matter most.

So, if you have a hard time thinking in terms of what it would be like to discover and live your unique purpose, think of that thing that calls to you like boats call to me. You just may find your best life and your passion in the place, the people and the causes that you feel drawn to. And, just like a sailor who catches the wind in his sail and finds his boat being effortlessly propelled forward, you will find your life being swept forward by a current of excitement and fulfillment that will exceed your wildest imagination.

So hurry to the dock and ... *Don't Miss Your Boat!*

– Kim Fletcher

INTRODUCTION

I magine having an opportunity to sit across from the person you admire most. You have millions of questions. The conversation is easy and comfortable, the kind you have in beach chairs as the sun sets. You find yourself wanting to find out the secret to the depth of satisfaction they have with life. What questions would you ask of them? What would you most want to know about this person who seems to embody authenticity, courage, creativity, adventure and clarity? The person you share this conversation with seems to have settled into their own life with a certainty that there is no one they would trade lives with.

You feel great just by being in their presence. You feel more alive than ever. It is as if someone just turned up the volume of your soul. Instead of a whisper, the deepest part of you is calling to you in a way that is clear and audible. Simply put, you find yourself wanting to take the next step into a deeper and more meaningful existence.

If that scenario captures your attention, then this book is for you! In fact, this book will allow you to become intimately acquainted with 35 people who have opened their lives and invited you in. These pages are filled with insightful conversations with some of the most incredible people you will ever encounter. However, they may begin to seem just like you and me. We call their stories a conversation because we don't want you to simply read this book. We want you to then continue the conversation by asking yourself what you can take away from their life journeys that will equip you to live your best life.

These are individuals who have searched for and found their unique life purpose. They have survived through, laughed through, and grieved through some ordinary and some extraordinary life circumstances. And most of all they have come through life with their hope, creativity, sense of authenticity, and the best of themselves fully intact.

It is our sincere hope that you will come away with a renewed commitment to discover and fully live your own unique purpose and passion, and that you will find yourself empowered to live your life with purpose in the real world ... YOUR world!

Let's sail...........

We relish news of our heroes,
forgetting that we are extraordinary
to someone too.

~ Helen Hayes

You Are Extraordinary!

Please God, Let Me Live

Travis S. Greenlee

It was a little over three years ago. I remember lying in my hospital bed feverishly listening to the rhythm of the pumps as they pushed chemo into my veins. What a strange sensation, I could literally feel the burning poison travel from limb to limb throughout my body. It started with my shoulder, then my chest and then into my stomach. I suddenly sat up and with an uncontrollable surge, vomited and began to cry like never before. In that moment, I realized that my life was out of control and that there was a good chance I wouldn't make it.

Yes, it was a frightening time in my life. I had just been diagnosed with Stage 4 Melanoma and was undergoing my first round of chemo. I realized I was in bad shape as I watched the tears fall from my dad's eyes when he videotaped my struggle. My dad has always been my hero… so strong, and so full of belief.

To see him in a place of utter pain and helplessness was overwhelming. Not knowing what to feel, how to react, or what to expect... I calmly slipped into a place I've never been before. It was surreal.

My mind raced... was I going to die or would I make it? What about my dreams? Would I have the opportunity to raise a family, build a business, and make a difference? I remember gazing out my hospital window to the park below. I watched the families play together, dogs running, children rolling around in the fallen leaves, and living life to it's fullest. I felt sorry for myself. Why, Lord, why me? What have I done to deserve such pain and fear? I'm only 34. I should have my entire life ahead of me. You see, up to that point, I felt invincible, as if I would live forever. I never really gave much thought to the possibility of dying before my parents, my friends, and my family. I acted as if I had all the time in the world to create my dream life. Not that I wasn't doing well. After all, I was successful in many respects. I had a wonderful job as a financial consultant and business advisor, an impressive title on my business card, drove a nice car, and lived in Newport Beach, California. I thought I had it all together. Looking back, I realize how small I had been playing. I had one foot in and one foot out of the door. I was sitting in the stands watching the game rather than stepping up to the plate and swinging the bat myself. I talked about my goals and aspirations, dreamed about them, yet never really took the steps necessary to allow them to unfold. Deep down, I guess I was afraid. Afraid of failure, and of what people might think of me. Afraid of taking a risk that might not work out. I was even fearful of becoming successful because of the added responsibility it would bring. What crazy thoughts.It was in that defining moment while drifting in and out of consciousness that I committed to designing and creating the life I had always wanted. One filled with love, peace, vitality, security, financial abundance, and unlimited opportunity. I resolved to follow my passion and purpose and make a difference in the lives of those I touched through coaching. Since then, life has never been the same. It's been a miracle and a blessing!

It's taken me three years of hard work to rebuild my life. From a health perspective, I'm feeling great! Better than ever. I'm riding my mountain bike, snow skiing, hiking, golfing, and working out on a daily basis and absolutely love it. Last year I fell in love with and married my soul mate Teresa. What a gift! We were fortunate to spend two weeks in Italy last summer, and spent our anniversary in Maui. We've decided that traveling to really awesome places works for us! We designed and built a new home in our dream town of Steamboat Springs, Colorado and enjoy an amazing community of loving friends. Our coaching practice continues to flourish and challenges thousands of people to enjoy more fulfilling lives.

So, how about you? Are you living the life you love? Are you enjoying a life filled with peace, happiness, joy, and abundance? Are you truly excited to be alive? The message of this story is very simple. It's important to realize how delicate and precious life really is. Your life is a gift from God that should be appreciated, nurtured, and cherished. Live each day as if it were your last, take the time to appreciate your many blessing and truly enjoy the moment. As you do, you will discover the miraculous.

Enjoy the ride. I wish you all the joy, happiness, and abundance in the world.

– Travis S. Greenlee
Business Design and Development Coach
President, Team Concepts Coaching
travis@teamconceptscoaching.com
www.teamconceptscoaching.com

Being Rich is Worth More than Money

Fred Knight

Had you ever stopped to think that being a parent does not really take much effort? Being a successful parent, however, is a whole different story.

The best advice my father ever gave me was the day he was holding my two month old son Jake on his knee. Jake was the first of my three sons, and this was the first time Dad had seen him. He looked me right in the eye and said,

"Son, it is your job as a father to teach this little guy everything you know by the time he leaves home."

I questioned him about this statement and he replied, "Teach him how to say thank you, how to change the tire on a car, to be kind to his mother, to use a hammer and saw, and to properly swing a baseball bat. Teach him how to talk to his adult superiors, to be polite, and to help an old lady cross the street. Take him to church and take him with you to work. Teach him how to build a fire and how to put one out. Read to him every chance you get. Tell him about the stars of the universe and the animals in the fields."

And on he went until I got his point. "But Dad," I countered, "That will take a lot of time. With work and all, I wouldn't have any free time left for myself!" "That's right. You are going to have to choose from now on what your purpose in life will be and what will take place as your top priority. If you spend all your time earning money, or doing activities by yourself, and ignore being a daily part of your children's lives as they grow up, you will be poor."

"Poor?"

"Being fabulously rich does not always mean one has a lot of money. Follow this advice and someday you will understand what I mean." he said.

And so I took his advice. When my sons were in first grade and went on their first field trips to the fire station, I took time off work and went with them. When they played little league, I never missed a game. When my youngest son pitched the final game of his high school career in the state quarter final playoffs, I was there to congratulate him on his win. Four days later when he and his team lost in the semifinals, I was there to share in his discouragement. By the time they had graduated from high school, I had used up all my spare time to teach them whatever it was I thought they should know.

As the years rolled by and the boys made the difficult transition into adulthood, I began to understand what my father had meant. We had three young men living with us who respected us, as we had respected them; talked with us as we had talked with them; included us in their activities as we had always included them. The peace of mind and stress free living that goes along with this type of family atmosphere is priceless, not to mention the satisfaction one feels knowing he has raised three well rounded, capable and knowledgeable human beings. No matter what line of work you're in, if you have kids, you 'gotta' be there. Maybe I could have made more money or traveled to far off corners of the earth. But at what price?

When I hear parents complaining about their kids getting into drugs or not wanting to communicate with them anymore, I have no idea how they feel for I never experienced those problems. If you make it your top priority to raise good kids, you will have good kids.

Proverbs 22:6 reads, "Train up a child in the way he should go: and when he is old he will not depart from it." Notice, it says to train a child in the way he should go, not the way he wants to go. This is of utmost importance! Follow this advice and you will know what it is like to be fabulously rich.

– Fred Knight
Dentist and Father of Three
fknight5@pe.net

"Expecting" The Unexpected

Chee Amy Vang

G od works in many ways...most are unexpected and have the most remarkable timing. Through knowing God, I have come to appreciate life in any given moment. I now understand that life is precious, and a gift from Him that lasts only a short time. I have learned to be at peace with myself even when my life plan has been shattered or turned toward the unexpected. A great life is achieved by what you make of it; not from what is handed down to you.

I learned this lesson from my parents who fled from China to Laos before I was born. The Hmong people, my people, were terribly oppressed by the Communist government, and were not permitted to become educated or to advance their lives.

I was born in a refugee village in Thailand during the Vietnam War after my mother and father literally swam to their freedom under heavy gunfire, crossing the river that divided their home in the country of Laos to the country of Thailand. Less than one year later, I was able to move to the United States where my desire to gain an education for my family and myself could finally be realized.

I married young, at nineteen, to a loving husband and gave birth to my oldest son two years later. No one in my family had ever earned a college degree so when the opportunity presented itself, I took it. My husband and I were both trying to make a living while attending college. I was fortunate to have my parents babysit our son as my husband and I worked to achieve our well thought out life plans. It was my last year of study to become a Physical Therapist Assistant at the local community college and I was looking forward to transferring to the University the following fall to pursue my master's degree. My life was proceeding as planned, with a great family and the hope of a college degree...and then maybe more children. I never anticipated having another child while dealing with the stress of college, work, and all the financial pressure that comes along with being a student, professional, and parent.

I remember it like it was yesterday. It was a hot and humid day in July as I stepped out of my doctor's office with a look of despair. My doctor had just informed me that I was two months pregnant.

For others it would have been a blessing, but for me, my life plan had just vanished into thin air...or so I thought. I struggled with the pregnancy knowing I would have to make many decisions regarding my career and family. My husband and I fought constantly because we felt we were not financially stable enough to support another child. He wanted me to give up college. I knew deep in my heart that continuing with my education would be the best for our children and us in the long run, so I refused.

Our denial of the pregnancy drove us to withdraw from one another when we needed each other the most. Being in denial diminished my focus on the truly important things in life. It wasted precious moments that could never be replaced. Denial can lead to poor decisions, unhealthy relationships, withdrawal, stress, and even suicidal despair, and we were on that path. I knew my husband's and my behavior were unhealthy, and I am thankful we had a positive support system in our family and friends.

Months passed and I had barely adjusted to the thought of one more child...when I found out that we were not having just one, but I was expecting identical twin boys. My hormones kicked in and my stress level increased. My cesarean was scheduled for March 17, 2003. I struggled to balance my roles as a wife, mom, student, and part-time employee. Finally, the big day arrived. I was taken back to the pre-operative room to prepare for the surgery. The surgery itself only lasted approximately eight minutes. After what seemed like decades in recovery, I was finally allowed to return to my room where my husband and two soft bundles awaited. Immediately, I fell in love with those tiny boys. My heart melted as I looked into those dark brown eyes. I knew instantly that my heart had been won over as they curled their tiny hands around my fingers. I had finally accepted my unexpected life plan...the life God had planned for me all along. I know now that acceptance is the KEY.

After a week of recovery from the twins' delivery, I returned to school to finish my last clinical. I graduated on time with my fellow classmates with high honors. From this experience, I learned that change is inevitable. I am a better person today because of the challenges I overcame and the compromises I willingly made. I did not allow the unexpected turn in my life to shatter my dreams or my passions. Instead, I was given something precious in return...a lifetime with my husband and my children, my true life purpose.

I will always have big goals and dreams, and I will always have the unexpected events of life pop up. Sometimes things happen that do not always fit into my life plan, but I know that wrapped inside of each event is a precious gift just waiting for me to open. I have a choice and you have a choice. We can accept the gift of the unexpected and experience the joys wrapped inside or we can become bitter, miserable, and full of frustration. I choose to expect the unexpected.

– Chee Amy Vang
Physical Therapist Assistant
Mother of Three
amyvangpta@aol.com

The Noble Awakening

Mary Enzweiler

Bad things happen to good people. One can waste time and energy complaining and mourning or focus on the realistic here and now.

On March 11, 2001 a bad thing happened to my brother, Kent. On this day, Kent, a gifted sub-3 hour marathon runner was training for the coming month's Boston Marathon. For the past 7 years, he and I had traveled to Boston to run the event. He, of course, completed the 26.2 miles much quicker than I; but nonetheless we both shared in our personal accomplishment of finishing. The 2001 Boston Marathon was to be no different. Wrong. On that Sunday morning in March, an out of control minivan careened onto the Cincinnati sidewalk on which Kent was running and struck him, catapulting him into the air, sending him crashing to the ground. He sustained serious broken bones and a more serious traumatic brain injury that left him comatose for the next five months. Due to these massive injuries, his doctor gave him a "less than 1% chance of leading a meaningful life." *Whatever that meant.* Miraculously, he has taken that slim percentage and has not only given meaning to life but has given our family, his friends, and me a new perspective of courage.

How can one seemingly shy guy who cannot remember his age, yesterday, or this morning's breakfast have such an impact on those close to him? The fellow who would say nothing as opposed to saying something derogatory about someone had suddenly and unexplainably touched a spot in each of us. An inexplicable noble awakening that had everyone wanting to do a "little something." Little things like visiting with a pizza, giving Kent a hair-cut or massage, allowing him to fire the starting gun at the Flying Pig Marathon, bringing him a vacation souvenir, paying his health club membership, con-structing a handicapped accessible addition to his house, treating him to an extra bagel at the local bakery, a lunch hour chat, downloading some favorite music, an e-mail from a distant friend, or a special hug at church. Separately, these were small thoughtful gestures ... collectively, they created a huge healing impact. Kent and I have truly been blessed with a wonderful family and we have chosen equally virtuous friends. I cannot speak for my fam-ily or his friends but I believe they share my feelings. I now realize that my independent single life is not "all about me." Everyone is vulnerable to catastrophe, we all need each other, and anyone can make a significant personal or societal contribution.

Since the day of his accident, I have been thankful to Kent for never having given up and to his friends, family, and caregivers for never giving up on him. How could I show my gratitude to all those who have helped Kent recover? I could not do it monetarily (I am not that wealthy) nor could I personally thank each person individually (there are far too many of them). I made a conscious effort to reprioritize my life and give back to Kent and to those who rallied behind him when he needed it most. I have found myself organizing fundraisers for Drake Center, Kent's rehabilitation hospital in which he spent 22 months slowly regaining physical and mental abilities lost in his accident.

When no other facility wanted to treat Kent as a patient due to his poor prognosis, young age of thirty-four, and projected care requirements, the Drake Center and its staff accepted, met, and exceeded the challenge. Once a frequent participant in the local running races, I now substitute running with volunteering at these events. I find it more satisfying in making a race a pleasant and safe experience for my running friends than in winning any age-group award. I still occasionally enter races, but now I silently dedicate my running to those that cannot. Remembering those five months of coma-like unresponsiveness and one-way conversations, I make it a point to have a daily conversation with Kent. Most of the time we talk about nothing in particular...we just talk.

Although Kent continues to use a wheelchair and is challenged by speech and cognitive impairments, his heart and spirit are as full as ever and maybe more so. He is an inspiration each day in which he defies that initial prognosis of "a less than 1% chance of leading a meaningful life." The once gifted athlete has now simply become 'the gift'. The rest of us accept the gift Kent gives and strive to become better people – meaningful people.

A family's history can more aptly be called a journey. When unexpected and catastrophic events force us to acknowledge the frailty of life, we all wonder–what should we do with the time we have? For my family it was to tell the world that Kent was here...and still among us. Dark days have now become days of glory and grace as we see Kent's influence on others. **His courage and goodness is how we hope to live.**

– Mary Enzweiler
cmaryrun@fuse.net

The Great Exchange

Renee' Parker

H ave you ever thought about how short life is or how quickly a moment can slip by? I have discovered that each and every day is a precious gift from God. He has great plans that I can't see for myself unless I gain His perspective and not simply rely on my own limited vision. Our perspective in life can either make us or break us, but it all comes down to choice. Each and every one of us is given choices.

I haven't always had the kind of attitude that you could say was a *blessing*. Actually, I was quite rebellious. I would have also argued with you that we don't always have a choice in life. So many times, I felt like a "victim", and believed that I couldn't change my life or my circumstances. The events about to unfold in my life became the catalyst that brought me to this realization; we do have a choice and our choices always affect those around us, either for good or for harm.

The choices made by a stranger, on a dreary March afternoon, totally changed the course of my life forever. His choice was to use a 38 caliber revolver to try to destroy as many lives as possible. Maybe he felt like a victim, too. He made a choice that day that left my boyfriend, Michael, lying on the ground paralyzed from the chest down, a bullet severing his spinal cord.

Suddenly, my life was not "all about me". I had some huge decisions to make. I had to determine where my strength came from and what I believed in. I failed miserably in my search for the answers to these questions, because I still had my limited perspective. What I really needed was to see through God's looking glass by taking on His perspective. Little did I know that it would be almost three years before I would find the real truth and meaning to life.

My strength and passion came from my rage, anger and bitterness. That is what kept me going when I felt like giving up. I can tell you that the very thing I lived off of, was eating me alive on the inside. I felt as if my heart had been torn into too many pieces to ever be put back together. Once again, I felt like a victim of the world, without hope and without a choice. After three years had passed, a friend invited me to church. The more I listened to the pastor and heard about God and His love for each and every one of us, my heart ached to have God's love on the inside of me! Even though I fought it, somehow I knew that what I was hearing about God was true.

The choices I had made in my past haunted me. Did this tragedy happen to Michael and me because of our past and our mistakes? So many questions and doubts plagued my mind. Guilt and shame were my constant companions, and I was so engulfed by my anger and bitterness that I didn't think my life could change. Then I realized, this shooter, a customer of Michael's father, made his own choice that day and was listening to the wrong voices. What happened to Michael did not happen because of my past or Michael's past. At the moment I embraced this critical truth, it was as if God himself reached down and lifted this huge weight from my shoulders and suddenly, I could breathe! The hope I had been looking for found me!! My life was totally transformed when I made 'The Great Exchange', trading my limited viewpoint for God's unlimited perspective and acceptance. My circumstances didn't change, but my perspective did. God gave me His eyes to see how short life really is, and that every day is a gift not to be taken for granted. Truly, life is not gauged by the length of days you are given, but it really is a matter of how you spend those days.

I came to realize that God *does* have a plan for my life. Jeremiah 29:11 says, "For I know the plans I have for you," declares the LORD, "plans to prosper you and not to harm you, plans to give you hope

and a future." The most important choice I have ever made is the one that has brought hope, peace and meaning to my life. Jesus is the answer to all my questions, even the ones I think have no answers.

God allows me to see a miracle everyday, my husband. Michael and I were married in October 1995. He is still in a wheelchair, for now. That's the amazing thing about knowing Christ. He truly has exchanged my limited vision with His higher perspective. He sees hope when I think there is none, and He gives me peace that this world could never offer.

– Renee' Parker
Professional Speaker, Vocalist and Writer
amazedbygrace2002@yahoo.com
www.geocities.com/amazedbygrace20022002

Bullets, Bats,
and a Bomb Shelter

Susan Vitalis

What would you think about if you had less than three hours to live?

That thought was far from my mind as an elementary aged child. That was when thoughts of becoming a missionary in a far away land began echoing in my mind and my heart. Later in college, I decided to pursue medicine as my career. And at some point along the way, those early dreams of becoming a missionary and my education as a physician began to merge into my greater vision for my life ... using my medical skills to reach and touch others in a significant way.

What began years earlier as only a dream and a vision had led me to this point in my life. The day was Thursday, March 3rd. It started like any other day in southern Sudan. As I stepped out of my tent, in awe of the brilliant sunrise, my thoughts meandered between my work at the clinic, how much the heat would increase as the day progressed, and what we would eat for breakfast. I did not realize this would be one of the most pivotal days of my life.

On my way to the clinic, I stopped at the feeding center to look for a translator but found it closed. Since there had been a near riot the previous day, the decision had been made to temporarily close the center to avoid complete chaos, with the intent to reopen in the afternoon. As it turned out, the feeding center would be closed permanently.

Eventually, I found a translator and we proceeded along the dirt path to the clinic as planned.

That was when the sound of gunfire began, changing everything.

It was distant at first, but it was definitely gunfire. As we had been taught, we radioed the U.N. base in Kenya requesting an airplane for evacuation.

The next three hours felt like three days. The gunfire increased in intensity as it moved closer to our village, eventually permeating everything around us. When the bullets began to pierce the trees over our heads, we decided to escape to the bomb shelter. As we dove into the bunker, bats whizzed past our ears on their way out. Apparently we were a greater threat to them than the gunfire.

While pondering the fate of the bats, I realized that I was likely to die that day. *Heaven is waiting, I thought. I am not afraid.* My most intense response concerned my family. We are very close, and I did not want them to have to deal with my death.

Soon the wounded were brought to our compound, so we climbed out of the bomb shelter to begin treating and comforting the injured as they continued to arrive. We were ill equipped for what we faced. Limited supplies made our task difficult. It was sobering and heart wrenching to look into the eyes of people I had grown to love and see a plea for help as they bled from gunshot wounds. One woman died as we desperately tried to stop the flow of blood from her gaping wound. She was one of twenty five who died that day.

Upon hearing our rescue plane approaching, we began running to the airstrip.

An ominous feeling oppressed everyone. As we ran through the village, I was surprised at the intensity of my mixed emotions. I was relieved to be escaping, but felt guilty for leaving people who needed my skills as a physician. I felt like I was abandoning this village I had called home for three months. I wanted to live, but what about the people left behind? They would also choose life if given the option.

Just when I thought that my heart couldn't possibly handle more emotion, Elizabeth, a Sudanese clinic worker and friend, ran to me with tears streaming down her face as she tried to hand me her young daughter. She loved her child so much that she was willing to give her away to keep her safe. *How could I tell her that I could not take her daughter? Or could I take her?* My gut instinct told me to keep mother and child together.

The plane never even came to a full stop. We jumped in while the pilot prepared for immediate take-off.

We later learned that we had been caught in the middle of a rival tribe's cattle raid. Two days later that tribe returned and burned down the entire village, leaving only charred tent poles and the bats safely back in their home, the bomb shelter. Questions concerning the fate of the villagers continue to be unanswered.

In the ensuing years I have struggled with my emotions when remembering that day, trying to make sense of my conflicting feelings. Why did I survive while so many others perished? Just as I left Elizabeth's daughter where she belonged, in the arms of her mother, I try to leave unanswered questions where they belong ... with God who fully understands and holds the answers.

I believe our challenge is to be all we can be now while we still have this gift of life, committing our unique passions and gifts to impact our world in a positive way, and to gratefully acknowledge all of those who support us and bring out the best in us as we seek to discover and live our true purpose. Not sure of your purpose? Well, what would you focus on if you only had three hours to live? The answer to what is truly important to you is likely found in that answer!

– Susan Vitalis, M.D.
Family Physician, disaster relief
Writer and Inspirational Speaker
svitalis@jhu.edu

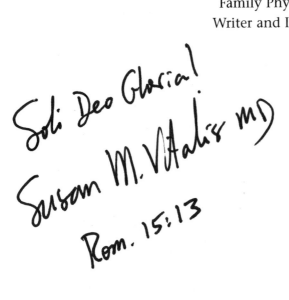

Soli Deo Gloria!
Susan M. Vitalis MD
Rom. 15:13

*How we spend our days is of course
how we spend our lives.*

~ Annie Dillard

Live Your Days Wisely

The Gift of Pain

Kathi Tunheim

In 1998, I was thirty-eight years old and director of leadership development at American Express Financial Advisors in Minneapolis. I had three young children, we had just built a new home, and my husband was a partner in his law firm. Life was good, busy and full.

That January, during a large conference in Phoenix that my staff and I had organized, I suddenly developed the worst headache of my life, a pounding pain that went away only when I was lying down. Even after returning home, I could not get rid of the headaches. Driving to work, the pain would force me to pull over and lie across the seats until I could continue. Soon after arriving at work, another headache would appear, forcing me to lie down on the floor of my office. As the day progressed, I could last only forty-five or fifty minutes until I needed to lie down again. Fear filled my head and heart. What was wrong with me? Why couldn't I get back to normal?

Yet my schedule was so busy that I couldn't seem to find time to see a doctor until my staff finally forced me to. After a series of tests—MRIs, CAT scans, and a spinal tap—I finally learned that I didn't have brain cancer as I feared, but I did have a hole in my spinal cord and most of my spinal fluid had leaked into my body. Lying down, what little spinal fluid I had left would travel to my brain and ease the headaches, but upright, the spinal fluid would drain out of my brain cavity, causing the piercing headaches.

My medical options were an extremely risky surgery or an extended period of bed rest in hopes that the spinal cord would heal itself. My physician at the Mayo Clinic told me bluntly that since there was no obvious physical trauma to my system, he could only surmise that my condition was my body's response to stress and that I needed to make some significant changes in my lifestyle.

I humbly called my boss and took a six-month leave of absence. Although being away from my accustomed schedule of commuting, work, kids' events, dinner, and more work once everyone else was in bed made me feel like a failure, the enforced rest did allow me to tackle the stack of books next to my bed that I had never quite found time to read. All of which, ironically, were about balancing one's work and family life. I read them all and more. After several months of reading and journaling, I found to my surprise that I actually welcomed being still.

With so much time for thinking, reflecting and wonder, thoughts in my head soon turned into ideas. Suddenly, the ideas were actually speaking to me, compelling me and encouraging me. "Could this be God speaking to me?" I wondered. "Kathi, I have given you many talents and gifts. Now I want you to leave your job and share those gifts with my church." Unable to escape this persistent thought, I was plagued with questions. "Why me, Lord? Why can't you ask someone else? What if I fail? How will we get by without my salary? Why me, now?" Yet the idea continued to repeat itself over and over.

As a first step, I began working with a counselor to understand why I had become such a workaholic. Why had I enjoyed being at work more than at home? Why had work given me a greater rush and sense of accomplishment? I knew that to heal physically and emotionally, I had to find answers to those questions. As the counselor questioned me about my family of origin, well-intentioned farmers and resort operators who had worked nearly all day every day, I recognized that I had simply adopted their work ethic and taken it to an extreme. Learning how to "be" rather than "do" was a scary process. I pledged that if I got better, I would consider starting my own business.

After four months, I began to get better. After five months, I walked a block and believed I might someday be normal again. At six months, I walked a mile and realized that I was going to get through this thing. I had the best summer of my life, playing with my children, going to the beach, spending time at our lake cabin, finally learning how to play and relax. Soon after, I resigned my job at American Express and started my own business. Just as God had promised six months earlier, my first organizational development client was a part of His church, Augsburg College, a Lutheran college near my home. After negotiating a retainer for a nine-month project, I was on my way.

I just celebrated my company's six-year anniversary, the most rewarding years of my career. Getting sick turned out to be the best thing that ever happened to me. I have learned to take care of myself first, for if I don't, I am no good to anyone else. In my new life, I am able to use all my gifts as a mom, a volunteer, and a professional. After years of so little balance between work and the rest of my life, I have become an expert on the topic, speaking nationally and currently finishing a Ph.D. in the field. This is a life issue that has chosen me. My experience with illness offered me an unexpected direction and purpose in life, to glorify God by inspiring servant leadership in others. From my greatest pain, has come my greatest offering to the world.

Today, I am the President of Tunheim Leadership Group, Inc. The mission of my company is to appreciate, educate and inspire leadership, team and organizational development to help others reach their God given potential. My purpose is clear and the gift of pain helped clarify that for me. Can you clarify your mission before a life-changing illness forces you to decide?

– Kathi Tunheim
President, Tunheim Leadership Group, Inc.
Leadership Consultant and Inspirational Speaker
Kathi@Kathitunheim.com
www.Kathitunheim.com

Walking Through Tar

Liza M. Shaw

Years ago a client told me, "Depression feels like being stuck in a black, sticky tar pit. The more I move, the more I get stuck." I empathized the best way I could as a young, inexperienced Marriage and Family Therapist. That statement was similar to descriptions of the disease I had heard uttered by many other such clients, and I made a sincere effort to understand the experience.

Although, at the time, I had never suffered any form of serious mental illness, I had definitely had my share of emotional struggles. Growing up in an alcoholic family had provided me with many opportunities to learn of the great suffering and pain that exist in this world. Rising above the adversity of my past, I came away from my childhood with a deep desire to make a difference in people's lives. I knew very early in my psychotherapy practice that I had found my life's purpose.

In these early years, I advised most of my clients in the same way. By implementing a widely used treatment for depression, I had learned during my professional training: Cognitive Behavioral Therapy. This treatment states that symptoms of depression can be alleviated by addressing the thought-patterns in the affected person. It is based on the belief that negative feelings are a result of unconscious thoughts about a situation. Change the thoughts about something and the feelings associated with it will change.

And so, I encouraged my depressed clients to begin paying attention to their "internal dialogue," the thoughts they have throughout the course of a day. I taught them various techniques to reduce negative thoughts and replace them with positive ones. Naturally, being the eternal optimist, I expected that the techniques would work – and sometimes they did. But often, I found that my clients were unwilling – or too stuck – to practice them and this I just didn't understand. I often became very frustrated. I saw the depth of their suffering, and I wanted so much to take away their pain. I felt like I knew the "answer" and they seemed unwilling to apply the knowledge I shared.

And then, I was presented with the most perfect, and yet painfully difficult learning experience. Two years into my professional practice, I went on maternity leave when I gave birth to my first child. Life as I had formerly known it ended when I was struck with a most shocking and debilitating case of postpartum depression.

I was totally bewildered by the feelings that overcame me. My child was beautiful, healthy, wanted and loved, and yet, day-by-day, I felt more hopeless, fearful and sad than I had ever felt in my life. Neither my husband nor I could believe that I could fall victim to this terrible mental disorder! Not after all that I knew and all I had done to help others! It was such an unexplainable feeling... to experience such deep despair for no earthly reason. The more sadness I felt, the more I worried. The more I worried, the more hopeless I felt. I often felt guilty about my sad feelings and then I felt guilty about feeling guilty! And if I ever experienced a moment or two when I didn't feel guilty, I felt guilty about that, too!

My negative thoughts were completely out of control, spiraling down in a vicious cycle. I began to truly understand what my clients had once told me about the tar pit. The more I tried to move in it, the more I got stuck.

During those difficult days, I remember wanting so desperately to be "delivered" from the suffering I was experiencing. I prayed, sometimes unceasingly, that God would take away my fear and pain. I just wanted to feel "normal" again. And then one day, I experienced what can only be described as enlightenment. It occurred to me that there might be something very significant I was missing.

Perhaps this experience I was having was a gift. "But how can suffering be a gift?" I argued with my inner voice. "The lessons you will take from it will change you," I heard from deep within.

And thus began my struggle back to myself. I confronted my pain, and realized that if I was going to not only survive my depression, but also *learn to thrive* again, I would have to "walk the talk." I pulled out my old textbooks on cognitive behavioral therapy, and got to work.

I used the many techniques I had taught my former clients to use, and I learned how hard it is to do what I had expected of them. I had been looking at the assignments I gave them as "homework," and judged them as irresponsible when they came back to me with excuses for not doing them. But this was not just homework – this was "life changing" work. It was the hardest work I have ever had to do. It meant not just daily practice, but minute-to-minute consciousness. The negative patterns which had become the default in my life had to be decimated, literally one thought at a time! It was a slow and grueling process of change. There truly was no quick fix.

I am not even sure when the change occurred, but over the course of two years, I began to feel lighter. I had more hope and less worry. I began to listen to that inner voice which reminded me to fear less, laugh more, and experience pure joy in the present moment.

I have changed in many ways. I have learned to be an optimist again by cultivating a grateful heart. I have learned to surround myself with positive people and situations, and to set firm limits around taking care of my needs. I practice the power of positive thinking, and have developed a deep faith in God that I depend on every minute of every day.

But the most important change has been the attitude I have towards the courageous men and women, boys and girls who enter the therapy room with me. I have a new respect for my clients that I never could have gotten any other way. I know the feeling of being stuck. I understand total hopelessness. It now makes perfect sense to me why someone would have a hard time making positive changes. It is like walking through tar.

The lessons my relatively brief illness taught me were invaluable. I now know, with total certainty, that the suffering my clients experience is part of the larger process that is their life. I know there are lessons for my clients as well. As a therapist, this gives me great peace, no matter how troubled my clients may be.

– Liza M. Shaw, MA
Marriage and Family Therapist
828-302-2978
lizashaw@charter.net
http://therapists.psychologytoday.com/33749

Dare To Step Out

Judy Siegle

In a split second in time, life as I had known it came to a screeching halt. I was involved in a car accident with a drunk driver the summer after my high school graduation in 1979. I was thrown from the car, breaking my neck and leaving me a quadriplegic, initially paralyzed from the shoulders down.

During a conversation with a pastor while still in the hospital, I broke down crying as I began to realize the full impact of my loss. He told me to imagine God so close to me that I could beat on His chest with my anger. And so I did, on more than one occasion! That helped me to move forward to meet the huge life change before me.

Growing up in Pelican Rapids, Minnesota, sports had been a big part of my life. In addition to being captain in basketball, cheerleading and track, I was an all-state basketball player.

Following my accident, working out daily was important ... I knew how crucial it was to have as much strength as I could for my daily activities. In the next weeks, months, and years, I worked to strengthen the muscle return I had been getting, allowing me to walk for short distances with crutches. I thought my days in sports were certainly over.

After 6 months of hospitalization, I began college. During my college years I became actively involved with Fellowship of Christian Athletes (FCA). I knew at heart I was still an athlete, even though my game had changed a bit!

One summer I worked as a counselor at an FCA camp with 250 high school girls. Each morning the girls were out for their morning competitions playing flag football, basketball, volleyball, etc. I remember sitting in my wheelchair and longing to be out there with them in the middle of the action. Then it dawned on me that I am uniquely created. In fact, none of us have the same muscle, hand coordination, vocal cords, mental capabilities, dreams or passions. We need to invest in who we are by developing the individual talents and abilities that we have been given instead of concentrating on what we aren't or what we can't do. We need to **dare to step out** ... sometimes easier said than done.

One such time for me was when I was learning to step up my walking from the gym into the real world ... the fear of falling threatened to stand in my way. It was one thing for me to walk in the safe and protected environment of the gym and quite another when my therapist said it was time to begin walking in public. I felt like a fish out of water when I was out of the chair! The chair had become a safe place, much like the gym, where I could be myself without the stress that came with the fear of falling.

As a college student, I would drop my book bag off at my desk, park my chair in the hall just around the corner and then I was up, seeing people eye to eye, walking in public. Even though I initially hated this activity, I found comfort in knowing that God knew my fears and would give me strength to meet this challenge.

Falling was one of my greatest fears at this stage in my life. Surprisingly, I rarely fell. How often in life do we have fears that are never realized ... fears of failing, fears of what others may think if our approach is unique or different? I had to learn that falling was not failing. Falling and failing were actually part of the process. It was in those attempts that I moved ahead.

I was developing an attitude of DARING TO STEP OUT and meeting life head on. As I did, new opportunities began to come my way.

What a thrill it was when doors began opening for me in the world of sports. Twelve years after my accident, I became involved in downhill skiing,

canoeing, kayaking, and quad rugby. Although I have not mastered all of these sports, the thrill for me is being out there doing my best. That is what I believe sports – and life – are all about.

Daring to step out led to several other accomplishments and opportunities. I am a two-time Paralympian (Atlanta, 1996; Sydney, 2000) and national record holder in several wheelchair track events. I have traveled to Romania to deliver wheelchairs to individuals with disabilities, and have a job that allows me to educate, encourage and challenge others using my life story as the catalyst.

As you give 100% today toward developing your unique gifts and abilities, I hope that you will dare to step out and embrace the opportunities that come your way!

– Judy Siegle
Two Time Paralympian and Motivational Speaker
Author of *Living Without Limits* (released in 2005)
Community Relations Specialist-MeritCare Health System
judy.siegle@meritcare.com
www.judysiegle.com

Infinity is as Far as a Girl Can Go™!

Natalie Petouhoff

*"The future belongs to those who believe in
the beauty of their dreams."*
– Eleanor Roosevelt

I remember how I passed the time waiting for the Comet cleanser to do its work. At age six, it was my job to clean the bathrooms. I discovered that if I wet the porcelain, sprinkled the cleaner on it, and waited a few minutes, the dirt would come off much easier.

The question was what to do with that time in between. Grabbing a hairbrush, I pretended it was a microphone. I watched myself chatting with the imaginary audience in the mirror, answering questions and giving advice. My mom passed by the bathroom and asked whom I was talking to.

I answered emphatically, "The people. Just telling them what they need to know."

She chuckled to herself and said, *"I know you can do whatever you dream of."*

It was my fantasy as a little girl to move to California and become a TV reporter and host. My parents nurtured my dreams as much as good parents do, but life had other plans for me.

I had been born into academia. My parents were sophomores in college at the time of my birth. Being an older student, my father preferred the social company of his professors, so I literally spent my early years being bounced on the knees of brilliant academics. My little mind could not help but absorb the conversations of these adults as they pondered the many questions that emerged from science, philosophy and the art of language.

When my family moved to Kentucky from Michigan, my parents did not have much faith in the school system in our new town. My mother had been a teacher, and she decided to hold "science class" each weekend for my siblings and me. For example, on Saturday, my family would go on a field trip to learn about manufacturing or an assembly process, like building a car or making bourbon. Other times, we would collect pond water and identify the amoebas and other strange, wiggly things in it. I quite naturally became fascinated by how the world worked. At the end of the day, I loved reporting to the family, along with my siblings, all that I had discovered. This was what was normal to us; we were a family of nerds, very happy nerds.

But the happiness did not last. In spite of all the good things happening in our family, my mother was diagnosed with cancer and passed away just before my fifteenth birthday. The day she died she asked me, the oldest in the family, if I would raise my siblings – two brothers and a sister, then aged two, four, and eleven, respectively. She was worried about what would happen to her babies after she was gone. In that moment, I was no longer one of them. I said the only thing I could, "Of course." And she closed her eyes and left for heaven.

Upon returning home, three sets of eyes stared at me. One needed his diaper changed, one needed help with his homework, and another just needed a hug. My father, faced with the grief of life without my mom, searched for solace in a bottle of vermouth.

And that is how I became a teenage "mom" – not through my own choice but through circumstances far beyond anyone's control. The dreams of the little girl in the bathroom were lost under piles of baby food, bedtime stories, baths, homework, laundry and cooking.

Fast-forward from that little girl to an adult: those dreams became buried even further under a difficult marriage and subsequent divorce, and a hard earned doctorate in High Energy Particle Physics. I had managed, through all of this, to move myself from Michigan to California – part of my dream began to see the light of day. I was now a professor at Pepperdine University's Business School, teaching leadership courses, working as a Life Coach, and writing books. The long awaited dream began poking its head out in an unexpected way. While I was no TV reporter, I was achieving an important part of the goal: telling people what they needed to know.

One day, many years later, I was visiting my father back in Michigan. We took a walk, although by this time he had a very slow gait because Parkinson's disease had taken control of his body. He looked at me squarely and said, "Mom told me the Comet story. I think you should do it."

"Do what?" I asked.

"Follow your dream. Become a TV reporter. You would be great!"

In the silence of our walk, the Michigan falling snow glistening in the moonlight, I began to see how my once forgotten dream would take shape. I remembered an opportunity I had to judge the "National Search for Inventors" contest. There would be a lot of national media coverage of the event. This was my first job on television. While my life had seemed to take twists and turns so far afield from my dream, it had, in fact prepared me well for this challenge.

All my years of adversity, accomplishing the nearly impossible as an inexperienced teenage "mom" gave me confidence. It was intimidating to appear on television. At first, I asked myself, *"Can I really do this?"* Yet self-assurance developed in me. Raising my siblings taught me that I could truly do what my mother had stated so confidently all those years earlier: whatever I dreamed of. My father reminded me that no matter how old we are or how long ago it was that we had a vision, dreams can still come true. After all, infinity is as far as a girl can go!

> *"In the presence of love, miracles happen."*
> – Robert Schuller

– *Dr. Natalie Petouhoff*
College Professor, TV Show Host
Rocket Scientist and Professional Speaker
doctorofchange@earthlink.net
www.drnatthetechnocat.com

The Finish Line That Was My New Beginning

Stacy James

It started out as another hot, beautiful summer day when a few friends and I decided to go swimming. I was nineteen years-old and a junior in college. Life was good. Without a second thought, I climbed onto my friend's shoulders in the shallow end of the in-ground swimming pool. I didn't know that it would be the last time I would ever stand on my own. A few seconds later, I dove off his shoulders into three feet of water and hit my head on the bottom of the pool, breaking my neck. While most of my body would be paralyzed, I was determined that nothing could paralyze my spirit.

Over the next few months and years, I learned what determination, courage, perseverance, and faith are all about. I learned to dress myself, write, type, and push my wheelchair to class. I continued on with school, and I graduated from college magna cum laude. In my free time, I even learned how to snow and water ski with adapted equipment. But I never dreamed that one day I could race in the New York City Marathon.

"Come to New York and do the marathon with me!" a friend, Mary, challenged me.

"I can't do a marathon!" I responded. "I can hardly push my own wheelchair. No way can I go 26 miles!!"

I had plenty of really good excuses. The biggest was that I only had 25% of my upper-body strength, and I couldn't even grip the wheels with my hands. And besides, I didn't have a racing chair. I had never done anything quite like this before, and I was intimidated by the vastness of New York City.

But I wondered . . .What if I could TRY? If I could go around the track once, then I could go around again. Four times around would be a mile. And if I could go one mile, then I probably could go two. I decided I would try. Since I didn't own a racing wheelchair, I started training in my everyday wheelchair. I pushed myself around campus, in the gym, and around the track. I was slow, but my muscles and my determination grew stronger with every push.

Since I wasn't physically strong, I needed to tap into additional strength if I was going to even attempt this. I remembered my favorite Bible verse, Philippians 4:13, "I can do all things through Christ who gives me strength." It became my motto as I trained.

Seven months later, on a cold November morning, I arrived at the starting line of the New York City Marathon with my mom and a guide. I had my name and number on my shirt, and a bright yellow sign that said, "I can do all things through Christ who gives me strength," which I hung on the back of my everyday wheelchair.

We started at 8:20 AM – two hours before the official race started, since it would take some of us many hours longer to finish the race. There were about 200 other runners with disabilities and their guides from the Achilles Track Club. I could feel the excitement in the air as did so many people who began cheering us on! The starting gun went off, and our pack of 200 started up the one-mile hill on the Verrazano-Narrows Bridge. In no time, my team was left behind. I knew I was slow, but I didn't know how slow. Thirty minutes later, we reached the top.

I had been pushing through the streets for a little more than two hours when the elite runners ran past us. And then for the next four hours, the 30,000 other runners ran by us. I felt tired and achy, and a bit overwhelmed. Spectators and runners yelled "Go, Stacy!" and some quoted my verse to me. Six hours passed, and I was at the 13.1-mile mark – halfway.

Three hours later, the sun was beginning to set, and I could feel the temperature dropping. The crowds were gone, probably all at home now, and I found myself wheeling over signs they had left behind. I continued pushing through the cold, gray, empty streets of Harlem, wondering if I could go on. My muscles ached and I was on the verge of giving up. I looked above me at the banner - 22 miles.

I stopped for just a minute to gather my strength. I visualized the finish line and remembered that everyone who finished would get a medal. "You didn't come this far not to finish," I told myself, and I remembered the verse on my back, "I can do all things through Christ who gives me strength." I gave it one more push, and then another.

Eleven and a half hours after beginning the race, at 7:30 that night, I crossed the finish line with my mom and my guide. "Raise your arms as you cross the finish line!" my guide yelled. I could barely do it. I strained as I lifted my aching arms in victory, and the few volunteers that were left hung a medal around my neck. It was the greatest accomplishment of my life.

"I'll never do this again," I thought to myself. "Take lots of pictures!"

But it wasn't my last. Since then, I have completed 13 marathons across the country. I'm happy to say that my everyday wheelchair has been upgraded to a handcycle, but I always wear that same yellow sign with Philippians 4:13 on my back.

That first marathon wasn't just a race; it was a lesson in life. If I can accomplish all this in a wheelchair, you can get through your challenges and reach your goals, too. We have to stop making excuses for why we can't do something and figure out how we can. The battle is often won in your mind.

Don't you dare let your "limitations" stop you!

– Stacy James
Director of Walking Victorious
Professional Speaker
614-889-5785
stacy@walkingvictorious.com
www.walkingvictorious.com

Never Too Young to Have a Purpose

Elysse Barrett

Most people don't know what to think about a young woman who is working to make a difference in the world – someone who is passionately living out a life of purpose every day.

I often wonder why it is that almost everyone seems to have bought into the misconception that you have to "be somebody" to make a difference in your church, your community and with those you love and cherish. I believe that you don't have to be taller, skinnier, and prettier, have more money, or drive a better car. In my opinion, you just need to be real and authentic. When it comes right down to it, I believe that you'll remember the things you did to make a difference in someone's life or the work that you accomplished that changed your community. It takes a little thought and motivation to find your purpose in life. My challenge to you is to discover your passion, talent and interests. Then go out and use those things to make a difference. A purpose will motivate you, it will help you focus your priorities and it will allow you to develop your potential like you could never imagine.

I'm nineteen. I've graduated from high school with honors, traveled all around the United States, had articles published in national publications, and spoken in front of presidents and high level executives from national companies as well as non profit organizations. Although I have a unique mission in my life, I am no one special. I didn't grow up with any special advantages and I definitely didn't grow up with money. However, I have a passion and a purpose. The work that I do has led me to develop my own ministry, write speeches and articles, work on political campaigns and organize events for national ministries.

We all can find an excuse to stay in our comfort zone. It is too hot or too cold, too cloudy or too sunny, we're too busy or too bored, too young or too old. The amazing thing that I have discovered is that there is never a perfect time to start making a difference. The longer you wait, the less time you have. I challenge you to start now. Today is the best day to discover your purpose and start pursuing it passionately.

Don't think that you have to give up your laptop and running water and travel to the deepest, darkest place in Africa to make a difference that will count. Most of the time, the best way to make a difference is right in front of you, in your own family, your workplace or your community. I have a friend who makes a difference in people's lives just by leaving her phone line open to give an encouraging word to others who might have had a frustrating or difficult day. A grandmother I know travels once a summer to "her" orphanages in Mexico bringing them much needed financial support that she raised from the quilts she makes and raffles. She also provides a place for men who have just been released from prison to call "home" until they get back on their feet. And, I just heard of a group in our community who makes clothes for babies who are born prematurely since no major clothing companies make that size. The possibilities for making a difference are endless.

Making a difference is not always an easy job, but it is the most rewarding one you can ever have. Nothing can compare to the smile of a homeless man you just gave a coat to, the victorious accomplishment of a child that just learned to read, or the hug of a friend whose burden you just helped to lighten. Sometimes, though, you have to persevere, keeping at it day in and day out. Sometimes it is monotonous and downright discouraging. And, sometimes you'll only feel like you are doing 'little things' but big differences are made up from lots of little efforts.

The most significant difference you can make in someone's life is to find your purpose in Jesus Christ and seek Him with all your heart, mind, and strength. You can live for Him every day, setting an example for the world to see. God will reward your faithfulness to Him as you live your life of purpose for His glory. As a wise leader once said, "Duty is ours; results are God's."

I see the difference I have made not only in the eyes of those in an audience I have spoken to, but every day in the eyes of my brothers and sisters. Look around you and find a place to make a difference. One of my favorite verses from the Bible says, "Let no man despise thy youth; but be thou an example of the believers, in word, in conversation, in charity, in spirit, in faith, in purity." (I Tim 4:12.) There is no age limit or time limit. We need to especially encourage children and young people to make a difference – they are the leaders of tomorrow.

You are never too young or too old to begin living your life with purpose. **When you do this, you will have ultimate hope for tomorrow.**

– Elysse Barrett
Age 19
Professional Speaker
President- America's Renewal
ebarrett@americasrenewal.com
www.americasrenewal.com

I think we're here for each other.

~ Carol Burnett

Can You See The Smile Of Those You Are Here For?

Why My Kids Are The Wisest Creatures I Know

Karen Helton

There were a million thoughts that ran through my head when I agreed to contribute to this book. Would I have anything meaningful to say? What could I write that might inspire someone else? These thoughts fueled the stress, worry, and insecurities that always haunt me when I have to put my thoughts on paper. In the midst of all this pondering though, was the constant presence of my three girls. Then I realized my inspiration was right before my eyes. My story would come in the form of curly hair, laughing eyes, and the small voices of my little ones that teach me every day. So take a minute to consider a unique world perspective from my children's point of view.

So here it is...

Be loud and persistent until someone hears you.

Being four-years-old has it advantages. You have every right to talk, insist, even raise your voice until your words are heard and your needs (or wants) are met. In childhood, this behavior is sometimes met with resistance. In adulthood, however, this ability can be priceless. I sometimes find myself squelching protests when I feel no one is listening to me, only later to regret it. Learning how to be more assertive and knowing how to go for what you want or need in life can be very positive and rewarding. So the next time you have needs that aren't being met, or you have ideas to share, find that four year old inside of you and make your voice the loudest in the room...figuratively or literally!

Five more minutes always make life sweeter.

How many times have we heard the phrase, "Five more minutes please?" or "Just a little longer?" and you were frustrated by the words? Life is lived at such a harried pace, buzzing from here to there and then back again with a thousand thoughts zooming through our heads. This mentality of savoring just a few more minutes is often left behind in childhood. One day, however, I granted my three-year-old's request. I watched as they were joyfully trying to cram all the fun into the precious moments that remained. It was during those stolen minutes that I saw the genius in letting our grown-up selves enjoy those extra minutes every now and then. Taking the time to just look at our work from a different perspective often creates new ideas and may even create a new spark for things that may have become a burden. I think of my girls every time I savor an extra cup of coffee or read just three more pages of a favorite novel before opening the door to my busy day. Take the time, and use it for yourself, so that you, too, can be more productive and more peaceful. Five more minutes may be all the time you need.

Play fair or don't play at all.

Playing fair . . . Do we really know what that means anymore? Sometimes kids have it right when they blurt out the phrase, "You better play fair!" How many times do we slight someone at work, intentionally or not, and consider it just another day's work? Playing fair isn't about games. It is about opening your mind beyond the norm to think about how you can use the small, changeable aspects of your life to impact others positively. Letting the person with bread and a frozen pizza go in front of you in line, taking credit only where it is due, and making sure that there is no scapegoat in any situation...that is playing fair. Seeing my ten-year-old show her younger sisters how to share and be kind is the example I try to fall back on. Life is full of "toys" - things we own, treasure, and can share; rewards, pleasures, and kindnesses we can pass on. Just opening our hands to let go of the greed and reaching out to others with our gifts...that is what I call playing fair.

Hugs cure everything.

From a child's eyes, I asked my oldest daughter to explain this to me. The following was her explanation. In life, we are to treat others with love, take their thoughts and feelings into consideration, and learn that painful mistakes are sometimes hard to avoid. "Hugging," however, can fix life's disappointments. "Hugs" can be words of praise, a simple touch when others are grieving, a tissue to dry tears, or an ear to listen no matter how trivial the situation may be. "Hugs" include forgiveness, humility, and love wrapped in arms that hold and eyes that understand. So, as my girls often do, just go up and give someone affection, a spur of the moment kindness. It takes nothing from you and leaves behind a genuine legacy of goodwill. It's the most precious thing we can give...a piece of ourselves wrapped in a lovely package.

These rules can sound so simple, but my experiences in life have taught me that the simplest tasks can sometimes turn into seemingly impossible obstacles. I have dealt with the stereotypes of being a teen mother, then a single mother, then an unemployed single mother. I have experienced labels - one right after the other - that can drag the mind and spirit down until hope is lost and purpose hidden in depression and fear. After years and years of trial and error, joy and heartache, I have learned that a childlike wonder can be the most inspirational gift we can present to ourselves.

So when my hope is floundering and I feel at a loss, I open my eyes and behold the wonders of my beautiful earthly angels. Three precious miracles sent here to change the world one smile at a time. **And when I look into their eyes I know that life won't just be all right...it will be amazing.**

– Karen Helton
Mother of Three
Aspiring Businesswoman
monkeejean@charter.net

Moving Forward

Monica Bascio

I've always considered the way I live my life to be pretty ordinary. Although I don't consider myself unique, most people seem to think otherwise. Could it be my medal-winning athletic prowess, or my ability to overcome a traumatic, life-altering injury? Or is it simply an attitude of believing that anything is possible? Perhaps it's just because I get up every day, smile, and work specifically towards what I believe is meaningful. Sure, obstacles get in the way, but for me, they're just another challenge. I live to show others that anything can indeed be possible. I believe I have been blessed to travel the world, achieve my life-goals and meet many wonderful people along the way.

In 1992, I broke my back while skiing near Lake Tahoe. I'm often asked for the gory details of my accident, but the story is not very glamorous. I took a jump, landed awkwardly, and my life changed forever. I now live my life from a titanium wheelchair as a

T12 paraplegic. After twelve years, I have grown accustomed to life as a person with a disability. I look at challenges as something to overcome, problems to solve. Obstacles are indeed universal, but how I've managed them has uniquely shaped my outlook, my outcomes, and outward expression of my life. My mission is to keep moving forward. I commit to taking action each day toward any or all of my personal goals in life. I believe we are what we do.

After my accident, my thoughts focused on what was next. I've never stopped skiing, or moving forward with my life, and have rarely let anything get in the way of my path. Some people find that phenomenal, but really, I still ski because it's fun, it's a challenge, and it gets me outdoors and into our great big, beautiful world.

Whether obstacles are big or small, mental or physical, they really can break down into simple factors each day. I persist to stay motivated. This drive comes from within and provides me with a great sense of achievement when I step back to look at how I've come so far from that one day on the slopes. Moving forward...

My time is split as an Occupational Therapist (OT) and as a Paralympic athlete. As an OT, I've worked with a lot of folks who could benefit from a new perspective on their lives. As an athlete, I have gained discipline in my own life. Both of my careers make it possible for me to share and model my passion and purpose with others.

I am fortunate that I am able to live my life with purpose each and every day. Life from a wheelchair occasionally bothers me and it can be downright inconvenient at times. However, I lead what I consider a pretty "normal" existence and I realize that the way I live with my disability - or any other problem for that matter - can have a positive affect on others.

I have discovered that living this way elicits admiration from others. The example people see in the way I live my life is a catalyst to make changes in their own lives.

Twelve years ago, I promised myself I would exercise regularly to stay fit, stay strong, and stay healthy. Back then I was challenged to take up handcycling as a means to fulfill that promise. That decision has served me well, and I've since won countless races, including the U.S. National Handcycle Championships thirteen times, the 300-mile Midnight Sun Race in Alaska four times, and the World Time Trial Championship in 2002. I made a commitment to the goals I had outlined for myself and have taken advantage of all resources available to me in order to achieve them. My personal philosophy is simply making a commitment to yourself, your goals and your dreams that can fulfill promises to bring great rewards. Moving forward...

Now, my goal is preparing for the 2006

Paralympic Games as a member of the US Nordic Ski Team. For athletes with a disability, reaching the Paralympic Games is as prestigious as any "able-bodied" athlete reaching the Olympic Games. For me, to compete at this level will be a great success in itself, and what is most important is this opportunity to face my challenges, work towards a purpose and achieve my goals. As I train for this event, I know that I will have numerous opportunities to share this perspective and model a purposeful lifestyle both with people internationally as well as those within my community.

Life is how you choose to live it. Perhaps I'm lucky to be able to appreciate my blessings in life: a great husband, Ian, two wonderful dogs, Frank and Jack, and a beautiful home in sunny Colorado, or perhaps I am just another girl in a wheelchair. In my work, in my sport, and even at home with my family, I have consciously chosen to believe, and remind others, that tomorrow is always another brand-new day. What will I do with the day? What are my plans for next week, and the week after? How can I insure my visions come alive? Each day in my life is an opportunity to do more, a chance to be successful, and to make a difference.

– Monica Bascio
Occupational Therapist
World Handcycling Champion
Member of US Nordic Ski Team
www.monicabascio.com

Fresh Purpose

Rachael Zorn

Our family spent most of our summer days out-side before my dad, Jim Zorn, went to training camp. Spending time in the yard was a way for him to relax from the pressure of each season as an NFL quarterback, and it was a way for our growing family to be together. My sister and I played while my parents maintained the yard. We had fruit trees, a vegetable and cut flower garden, a huge lawn, and a massive rose garden. My dad spent the majority of his time in the rose garden pruning, killing aphids, and pulling weeds. As a seven-year-old, that 70 bush rose garden looked like a magical forest of color and fragrance, but the fairy tale ended when we had to weed and lay bark in it every summer.

A fresh new pile of bark sat in the driveway on one particular summer day, and I knew that spreading bark was easier than pulling weeds. I looked longingly at it while pulling weed after weed. I asked my dad why we had to weed the whole garden when we could just spread the bark and magically cover the weeds. He taught me that if they were not completely pulled out, the weeds would grow back through the bark. This simple gardening lesson became a life lesson that I would never forget.

Covering up weeds with bark is like covering up conflict in relationships. Problems, just like weeds, grow through the "bark" if not pulled out by the roots. I understood this as a seven-year-old when relating to my sister and my friends. I understood that if my sister Sarah and I didn't work through our fight, then the "weed" would still be there during the next fight. The same principle applies in my adult life. Covering up unresolved, unforgiven relational issues prevents relationships from remaining current, vibrant and alive.

But as I got older, I noticed that it became easier to cover up conflict with time, silence, anger and space. It was effortless, and almost natural to let a relationship slide. The more I avoided a specific conflict, the more I allowed resentment and anger to develop into bitterness. Bitterness if left untended, hardens and hollows hearts, and makes for a life void of love and joy.

I left college thinking I had finally "arrived" at a place of maturity and independence. I wanted to prove that I could make it and be successful in the "real world." With that attitude, I left a lot of friendships shipwrecked because I wanted to prove that I did not need anyone. I desired to make it on my own. After about a year, much of what I held on to tightly was stripped away - job, relationships, phone calls, e-mails, companionship, and purpose. I felt like a fish swimming in a fish bowl watching the world being lived all around me, and wondering when I would get to join in. I was empty. The bark I had been using to cover up my life had been blown away, and I saw some weeds that needed to be pulled.

I needed to reconcile some friendships that had died because of some weeds that I had ignored. One friendship faded because of jealousy. Everyone liked my friend and gave her the attention because she was fun, outgoing and cute. I felt that I could not compete, so over time I cut the friendship off. After college, she moved to a different state and never talking to her again would have been easy. But living my life alone in a fish bowl made me realize how rich life is when lived in relationship. Over coffee, I admitted that I was jealous of her in college and I apologized for letting the relationship slide. She forgave me, and two years of jealousy, conflict, silence and space became a freshly weeded garden.

With proper care and attention, my relationships keep me going and give me a sense of purpose. They motivate, encourage, challenge, and change me. But maintaining a relationship is time consuming, exhausting, and frustrating at times. It takes sacrifice, service and humility to keep a relationship healthy and alive. When I am most discouraged, lonely or wallowing in self-pity, I can usually attribute it to some unresolved conflict. Unsettled and avoided conflict always grows through the "bark" of life. It is difficult to humble myself and apologize or confront a friend about an issue, but resolution always deepens the relationship and allows me to move on.

It is often difficult to pull the weeds, but living life with current relationships that are nurturing and fulfilling gives my life fresh purpose that far outweighs living with weeds.

– Rachael Zorn
Seattle, Washington
rzorn10@yahoo.com

Welcome to My Life

Joshua George

Welcome to a moment in my life. A moment of reflection is in order when I realize how fortunate I am for the life I have. It's 8:30 PM, and just two days before I am about to go to Greece to race in the Paralympics, the biggest sporting event of my life. Parallel to the Olympics, the Paralympics is the premier international sporting event for people with disabilities. It has been a life-long goal of mine to make the games. I can remember the day I qualified for the U.S. Marathon Team. It would have been impossible to wipe the grin off my face! I have a million things to do before I leave, and all of my clothes are strewn haphazardly across the floor of my friend's bedroom. Due to the untimely expiration of my summer apartment lease, I have been living out of a suitcase for the past month. It hasn't mattered much to me though because during this time I have been working out an average of four hours a day and spending the rest of the day in a neanderthalic daze on the couch or in a lounge chair trying to recover. I have loved every minute of it.

My life has not quite paralleled what one might call a "normal" life, and I have never tried to make it one. When I was four-years-old, my life took an unfortunate plunge. I was walking on my apartment bedroom window sill attempting to reach a toy that had been out of my grasp. The next thing I knew, I was laying in a hospital bed with tubes sticking out of my nose, arms and chest. In my attempt to retrieve the toy, I had leaned backwards against the open window, popping out the screen, and sending my then tiny body hurtling to the ground from twelve stories up. From that moment, my chances at a "normal" life literally went flying out that window! One second I was a healthy platinum blond, giggling kid, and the next the doctors were telling my parents that I probably would not survive. Since I am sharing this moment with you, I obviously did survive, but with a spinal cord injury that left me a paraplegic, paralyzed and unable to walk. As strange as it might sound, I wouldn't by any means call it a tragedy. It was anything but that. I was on the front page of the Washington Post. I made all the local news programs, and I had my own set of wheels well before any of my friends got their first ride. My friends all thought it was cool because they got to be on TV too.

Thanks to my parents, my accident really didn't change my everyday life very much. I was just a naive kid who didn't understand why being in a wheelchair might be any different than not being in a chair. After surviving the brunt of my accident without any grey hairs or heart attacks (at least not any that I knew about!), my parents treated me the same as they had before. They never let me feel that I couldn't continue having fun or accomplish what I wanted to achieve simply because of my wheelchair.

I took that lesson to heart. Every decision I made was because it was what I wanted to do, and not because it was what someone else thought I should do. I began competing in wheelchair racing and basketball. I loved sports and I kept making the decision to take my athletic career to higher and higher levels as the opportunities arose. My wheels were in motion and nothing was going to get in my way.

At this moment, I have no regrets. I have never looked back with sadness at what I chose to give up so that I could compete. I missed a couple homecoming dances, a junior and senior prom, and numerous other high school events because of competitions, but it never felt like much of a sacrifice to me. Don't get me wrong, I had a few good friends in high school, and it might have been fun to go to a couple of those events with them, but I never lost sight of doing what I loved most.

The fun times in your life must outweigh the lackluster times. My magnificent ride on this planet is only going to last so long, and I will definitely want my money back if this ride drops me off at the end thinking, "Ok, now what?" It is a relatively simple concept; if you're not having fun in life then something is wrong. The word fun, though, has to be defined by you and you alone. Fun is not always doing what someone else has already done in their so-called "normal" life.

So, now I am about to embark on one of the greatest athletic journeys anyone can ever hope for. I am on the U.S. Wheelchair Track Team and am going to Athens, Greece to compete in the Paralympics. By doing something that has consistently made my life a blast, I am racing to Europe. I'm taking a semester off from college—oh yeah, racing and basketball also led to a partial scholarship at the University of Illinois—and am traveling the world having fun.

What's next? I don't really know. But this much I do know. I will continue rolling on with a big smile on my face, living life my way, looking for new adventures, and always having lots of fun.

– Joshua George
Two Time Paralympic Bronze Medalist
Student Athlete- University of Illinois
Sports Journalist
jgeorge@uiuc.edu

True Faith Confession
of a Hairstylist

Nina Heck

"I have decided I want to become a hairstylist," I announced proudly to my Mom and Dad. As a sophomore in high school, I thought I was mature and in control of my future. Little did I realize that I wasn't the one in control at all ... God was!

I had gone to church my whole life, but it wasn't until the year I turned sixteen that I began to develop a personal relationship with God. I started seriously reading my Bible and searching to know who God was and why He cared so much for me. It would be much later in my life before I would see the true reasons why God had led me into this career.

After graduating from cosmetology school, I was offered a job at a wonderful salon in the local mall. It was at that mall that I met the man of my dreams. Just a coincidence some might think, but I know it was part of God's plan for my life. After dating for just over a year, we were married. This would become my first and most meaningful purpose in life ... to be wife and best friend to my husband, and later to be a mother to our children. What a blessing and a great responsibility to raise children in our world today. This purpose has given me more joy than I could have ever imagined.

During the years that I worked in this salon, my professional experience grew, and so did my clientele. Along with many faithful customers came a desire to start my own business. My mom had her own hairstyling business and offered me the opportunity to come and begin my own business while operating out of her salon. I jumped at the chance. Her salon was located in the basement of the home I grew up in and was in a great location for developing my business. 'Returning home' was the perfect professional situation for me at this time.

Thirteen years later, after forty years in business, my Mom began thinking of retiring. This would mean closing her salon, leaving me with the challenge of finding a new location and the chance to open my own salon. A great location became available but by the time I made the contact, the space had been rented. In my disappointment and still working from my parent's home, I wondered what was next for me.

Then November brought a day I will never forget. I remember my dad, a quiet man who rarely complained, remarking that his back was hurting. He had been plagued with back problems through the years and was sure the pain was just a pulled muscle. But when the pain began keeping him awake at night, he went to the doctor. Muscle relaxers failed to relieve the pain, so the doctor ordered several tests to be done at the hospital. Our greatest fears became reality when a tumor was found. Once again, I discovered God's real purpose for me. By placing me back in my parent's home to work, God had given me the opportunity to help my mom care for my dad during the short six months before cancer took him to be with the Lord. These were some of the closest times I ever experienced with my father. I will forever be grateful for those last precious months with him … months that would have been impossible if that 'ideal space' for my salon had been available. I grew to be thankful that I had received the fateful call that my business could not relocate just two weeks before I learned of my dad's cancer.

The very week that I returned to work following my dad's funeral, I received a phone call letting me know that the same location that I once had looked at and loved had become available for rent. My purpose for working at my parent's home was fulfilled and now God was leading me to a new location, a new beginning.

Some may think, "I can see real purpose in being a wife and mother, but what great purpose can you find in being *just a hairstylist?*" I once wondered that too, but I have come to realize that God uses us if we are open and available to Him in all areas of our lives. If you have ever doubted that God could use you or your position in life for any real purpose, I challenge you to let the words of I Corinthians 1: 26-29 encourage you. Once you realize that God places you in your daily circumstances for a reason, your life will take on even greater significance.

My clients have become my extended family. We have laughed and cried together, shared joys and sorrows, and talked about much more than 'just hair' during our time together. It has been a blessing for me to be in a position to get to know and hope-fully make a difference in so many people's lives. I feel that my job, my real purpose, is to encourage and care for the people God places along my path in this life. Hairstyling is just a little something I do on the side.

– *Nina Heck*
Mom, Writer, Hairstylist
Hickory, North Carolina
828-294-4325

Thud

Jeremy NC Newman

*"If the only prayer you say in your whole life
is 'thank you,' that would suffice."*
– Meister Eckehart

My first love has always been the thrill of a challenge. As a personal trainer, athlete and self-professed adrenaline junkie, I've lived my life with competitive fervor and, more often than not, reckless abandon. I believed that even the law of nature – gravity – did not apply to me. I was an avid high school and collegiate athlete. My fitness routine consisted of at least two workouts per day. Riding motorcycles, cliff diving, bungee jumping, living on the edge and taking on any challenge were my life's blood. I believed women worshipped me; I thought I had the body of a Greek god. I was a strength and conditioning coach and had completed two marathons. Physical activity was my purpose. Life seemed good.

However, that same competitive fervor is what brought me to the brink of death. It was on May 24, 1997. I was a well-trained and experienced skydiver. Preparing for the jump, I was determined to beat my fellow skydiver to the ground. In that instant, I had my life's utmost competitive moment. While descending, I chose to partially collapse my parachute to beat him to the ground. In my mind, gravity did not apply. I won that race to the ground.

It was also a race I lost. In that moment, I made a decision that would alter the course of my life. I plummeted to the ground from twelve hundred feet. THUD...My body was paralyzed.

My heart stopped several times. The doctor who saved my life was told by his colleagues not to resuscitate me; I would have no quality of life. He did not listen. With the same fervor I had in life, he continued CPR. I was brought back to life. My doctors made grim predictions that I would never breathe, speak, or walk on my own again. The hospital staff prepared my family and friends for the inevitable. Some were willing to accept this – but not my family.

Despite my arrogance, my family loved me. They visited every day. They felt it was vital to talk to me, even though I could not respond. They felt it important to massage my limbs, even though I could not move. They wanted me to remember

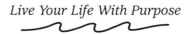
what it was to feel.

In my second month of hospitalization, I was faced with another life-altering choice. My mother watched helplessly as I pushed everyone away - my family, friends and hospital staff. Realizing I was headed towards self-destruction, she looked me straight in the eye and said, *"You can sit in this hospital bed and live the rest of your life being angry, bitter and alone or choose to create something positive from this."*

The next morning something miraculous happened. I could not control my bowels and therefore had an accident in bed. A nurse came to clean me up. I was embarrassed, so I yelled at her to hurry up. She looked at me and said, "I don't have to put up with this." As she walked away without finishing, the words of my mother resounded in my mind.

Many who have experienced serious accidents often speak of their lives as if it occurred in two parts: the before and after. In that moment, my mother's words rang so loudly in my ears, the sound was deafening. I had a choice: allow my spirit to live or to die. This choice, like all others, would again alter the course of my life. It is the choice we are all faced with, to be accountable for ourselves and how our actions impact us and the world around us. No challenge would prove greater than this one.

Shortly thereafter, I began to regain my mental and physical abilities. Doctors described my recuperation as totally miraculous. I was released in two-and-a-half months and returned to work the very next day. I have never looked back.

Being paraplegic did not prevent me from returning to competitive sports. With borrowed racing equipment, I began competing as a wheelchair athlete in the 1998 Los Angeles Marathon. I have since competed in dozens of marathons, triathlons, duathlons, and 5K and 10K races. In Colorado, I relearned downhill skiing as a disabled skier. June 7, 1999 – two years and two months from the day I "hit the ground" – marked the successful completion of my participation in the fifty-six day, thirty-six hundred mile Transcontinental Triathlon from Santa Barbara, California to New York City.

Now, as one of only two wheelchair triathletes on the U.S. National Team, my desire is to empower others to exceed beyond their perceived possibilities. I have traveled the world to Italy, New Zealand, Mexico, Switzerland and Portugal for speaking engagements and competitions. Most recently, I won the silver medal at the 2004 World Triathlon Championships.

I have learned to cherish all that has been given to me. I recognize all that I used to take for granted. For instance, simply taking a breath on my own means everything to me. Every morning when I wake, I say, "Thank you." Having taken myself to

the brink of death and returned with the gift of inspiration, my desire is to share this story so that anytime we think we can't – *we can.*

> *"The Impossible Just Takes a Little Longer"*
> – Art Berg

– Jeremy Newman
USA Triathlon Team Member
Motivational Speaker
Strength & Conditioning Expert
Touch, Move and Inspire
818-652-5542
thud@jncn.net
http://marketplace.getitplanet.com/website/JNCN

You can impress people at a distance,
but you can impact them only up close.

~ Howard Hendricks

Take A Step Closer
To Someone

Top Down Life

Kim Fletcher

"Life is either a daring adventure or nothing."
– Helen Keller

I have always liked having the wind in my hair, whether on skis, in a boat, or in a convertible. On the contrary, I have never understood people who tolerate hairstyles that take hours to put in place and lots of energy to maintain. My friend, Tammy, is the leader of that sub-culture … people who consider the wind the arch enemy of their hair.

I had a convertible years ago, 1991 to be exact. It was a cute little red Miata, a pint-sized car built for two tiny people who like to travel light … I had fun looking at it, riding in it (with the top down of course), and even keeping it clean. My dad says it is the only car I ever kept clean. Life was just different when I had that car. The simplest trip became an adventure. I have even been spotted with the top down and the heater blowing full blast, driving in snow flurries, dressed for an Alpine weekend.

Then came the Volvo wagon. If I were an artist (well, actually I am), I could call this my 'safe period'. The wind gave way to safety and practicality. 'You might just need the space for the extra six people and their cargo', chided the voices in my head. As a single gal who prefers being with one friend at a time, I now wonder why I listened.

The contrast between my 'adventure period' with the convertible and my 'safe period' with the station wagon parallels an interesting contrast in life. I am going to suggest that some of us live stuck in our 'safe years'. We concern ourselves with the agenda that others think best for our lives. We live on the safe side of our ultimate level of integrity simply because people expect less of us there. We settle for the status quo. We start to believe that we don't need to try harder when a high standard of excellence seems to be a dying art. We never quite tap into our brilliance, continuing to do things that aren't fulfilling rather than investing more time and energy into using our natural gifts and pursuing our passions.

When we choose the safe ride, the scenery is limited and the adventure is curbed by our desire to always be protected. We protect ourselves from failure by never taking the risk we really hear our heart calling us towards. We keep significant people who would greatly benefit our lives at arms length. But, like me, don't you find that life takes on another level of value and richness when we choose to take those healthy risks?

Tammy occasionally tossed her 'hair caution' to the wind and decided to ride in the convertible. I believe she would tell you that it was worth the consequences. We need to do the same with life. Just as hair gets messed up, life can get a bit messy too. Adventure and messes often share the same address, requiring us to put up with the inconvenience of one for the benefit of the other. Just as the owner of the highly guarded hair never knows the great adventure of the 'top down ride', the person with the closely guarded heart and life never knows the great adventure of the 'top down life'.

My tiny topless car was not the safest vehicle I ever owned. The way I currently live my life is not the safest way I have ever lived. In the past couple of years, I have chosen to follow my heart and redefine many areas of my life. I left a well-established career that I enjoyed as a physical therapist and college instructor to pursue my passion of investing in others as a professional life coach, author and speaker. I gave myself permission to let go of some relationships that were not positive influences. I made the decision to live a life of authentic faith. In short, I am learning that with healthy risks come great rewards and deeper discoveries of who God created me to be.

God actually reminds me of the wind at times. He blows into our lives offering the adventurous pursuit of life. He intends us to have a life that hugs tightly to the curves of personal excellence and integrity. He offers a willingness to love even in the midst of our deepest hurt. Life sometimes hands us broken relationships, failed professional pursuits, detoured dreams, and crushed hearts. It is at these crossroads that we must make the critical decision ... play it safe and avoid the wind, or jump back into life, wind and all.

I never quite got over parting with the little red, highly inconvenient means of transportation. I recently made a decision to scrap the safe ride and return to having the wind in my hair when I purchased another red convertible that is almost identical to the original. It is my hope that you will grab hold of adventure and authentic faith with me, wait for a great gust of wind, and enjoy the ride of your life. Get out there, put the top down on life, and turn down the winding road of the unknown to develop in yourself all you were created to be. The same wind that messes up your hair and shakes up your life also leads to the greatest adventures.

– Kim Fletcher
President, Creative Life Navigation
Life Coach, Professional Speaker
Advocate for Persons with Disabilities
www.creativelifenavigation.com

Dream With Passion

Dorothy Hobert

I have learned that you can do or be just about anything you dream. By setting your goals and plunging ahead without fear, you can make your dreams come true.

My mother taught me this lesson well as a woman who has made her dreams a reality in spite of many obstacles. When she was only fourteen, she lost her mother and was given the shared responsibilities of helping to raise four younger siblings. When she married, she had her own family of six kids. I watched in awe as she loved each one of us, worked nights, went to school days to become a nurse, and received her diploma with passion and joy.

My heart's desire is to be like her. For just like my mother, the joys in my life have everything to do with passion. I am proud to say that I have worn many different hats in my lifetime. I have been a wife, mother, and have been blessed to have three "jobs" that I consider not only jobs, but also means to fulfilling my purpose in life, living my dreams with passion.

I have done one of these "jobs" for over 35 years now. Perhaps my belief that every woman needs to feel beautiful is the reason why I've stuck with being a hairstylist and salon owner for so long. Sharing the good times and bad with my clients, I have made a difference in their lives as they have in mine. With every new cut, style and blow-dry, I am able to touch a life and live my dream with passion.

I almost lost sight of my dreams when I, like so many other women, became a divorce statistic. Those early days, when I faced the death of a 28-year marriage, were some of the darkest and loneliest moments of my life. I felt as if my Cinderella life had come abruptly to an end and I was lost in the black, stormy clouds of despair.

I spent months trying to recover, and I am so grateful for family and friends who stood by me, loved me and encouraged me to seek counseling. I emerged from the dark a changed woman who saw blue skies, glorious sunshine and a future once again filled with beauty and promise. The most difficult time of my life turned out to be for the best. I was ready for a new beginning.

During the time I was going to recovery meetings, I met a woman who would rekindle some of my buried dreams. With her guidance and help, I undertook the daunting task of sorting and organizing thousands of family pictures I had stored in boxes. The process of looking at each and every family photo was a therapeutic endeavor.

Because of this new experience, I decided to become a Creative Memories™ Consultant. I've had the joy of working with many families, helping them preserve their precious family memories. For the past eight years, I have been conducting classes and workshops, teaching others how to create albums and journal their family stories. With each photo and each life I touch, I am living my dreams with passion.

Doing what I loved each day filled my life with peace and contentment, but the reality of the divorce left me with considerable financial worries. I had no job related benefits, no steady outside income, and I wondered just how long I could make it on my own. I knew that if I was going to survive, I had to work smarter.

The smarter opportunity arrived when my sister-in-law knocked on my front door Halloween night in 2001. On that "spooky" night, she took a few minutes and introduced me to a line of products that were safe, without toxic chemicals, and had great financial potential. I enrolled that night to become a wholesale customer. After using the products for a short period and seeing the difference they were making in my life, it didn't take me long to introduce others to the benefits of a safer, healthier way of life for themselves and their loved ones.

As a marketing executive for The Wellness Company, my life has changed both physically and financially. I now have freedom to work when and where I choose. I am healthier. I have more time for family and friends. I can travel and fully enjoy life. My goal each day is to help others see a way of life they may never have thought possible. And with every new customer and business associate, I continue to live my dreams with passion.

My mother and my life have taught me many lessons. Some have been a little tougher than others, but they have all worked together to bring me to this amazing place in my life. I would encourage each of you to listen to your heart. Don't be afraid to take a risk and find the paths that will make your dreams a reality. Step up to new opportunities that can change your life. I wish for you to be blessed, and for you to know that you are special and unique. Refuse to let another day go by that is not filled with pursuing your dreams with passion.

– Dorothy Hobert
509-926-6343
katie_hobbit@hotmail.com
www.dorothyhobert.healthy2wealthyteam.com

Sunrise – Sunset

Dianne Hough

I am fifty-six-years-old and, for the first time, I am watching the sunrise – not with a group of would-be adventurers – not on the very first day of the year with a troop of exchange students – JUST ME. Well actually, Kodiak, my old and limping Alaskan Malamute is lying here beside me. His lamb fleece coat contrasts with the steely frozen patio we are seated on. I have my creature comfort as well . . . gourmet coffee with a douse of hazelnut creamer. Life is good.

This moment is particularly remarkable because I generally consider myself to be a "night hawk." I often stay awake into the wee hours of the morning and have consistently done so for most of my life. This early morning stuff (pre-dawn no less!) is new and strangely calm. How interesting that I even *like* this. Chaos is my usual way: wild, exhilarating chaos, and I'm usually the leader of the pack. Old cheerleaders never stop – they just cheer on and on.

Various family members have even teased me. My daughter called me a few years ago with a new, exciting discovery: "Mom, I just saw this show on TV," she said, "and I know what you are . . . you're a chaotic thinker!" It was as if she and the rest of my family had been searching for the answer to my crazy condition for years.

Asleep inside is my father, whose seventy-eight years have finally started to catch up with him. His dementia keeps him just out of reach most of the time. But the occasional moments of clarity with dad strike a rich and precious chord – like last night, when he declared, "You know, Di, *this is* what's important. Havin' the kids here and tryin' to make a bunch of fun."

My younger sister, Jeanette is also here with us. She brought her two children, Ben and Kelsey – who of course, *used* to be young. Now, suddenly, Kelsey has "painted" eyes (Dad thinks they're "magnificent"), and Ben races down the hills like a dare devil with his pants clinging to the last inch of his behind! My husband, Bob, is also quietly sleeping away in our bed as I sit here and do nothing. We literally are lost in a chapter of *On Golden Pond*. I look nothing like even an old Katherine Hepburn sitting here in my jammies and shades.

Kodiak hasn't moved. This morning stuff is too rich for him and he's just lying here waiting for the sun to heat up his chilled body. He's old too – and magnificent like Kelsey's eyes – but with a bad hip he has to drag around with him. Right now, he seems completely oblivious to it all. No pain, just presence.

The serenity that punctuates this moment stands in great contrast to the last twenty-four hours with my family in this mountain cabin by the lake. I had an idea for a "photo opportunity" with my near-senile father. I suggested that Bob slowly pull him around the cove on the back of our jet-ski. Apparently, the two had much braver ideas. They sped around the cove so fast I barely believed my eyes! Dad clung to Bob as they cornered their way around the bend, and then they were gone. At first, I was terrified. "He is going to kill my dad!" I thought to myself. After all, my father is usually connected to an oxygen tank! Well, I guess they just didn't have a long enough hose that day.

When they returned, everyone erupted in great roars of delight. Dad marched off of that "sea going vessel" as though he had just conquered the world – much the same way I imagine he did as he departed his submarine from World War II. Bob was full of pride for his father-in-law, declaring that an "old Navy guy" like Dad wasn't afraid! He had seen a lot more speed than that in *his day*. The male-testosterone thing typically impressed Ben. He was ready to jump on that jet-ski and capture some of the energy left out there on the lake!

Jeanette obviously had difficulty enjoying the

moment. She's into peace and tranquility - not speed! After a cigarette to calm her nerves, she was just fine. Kodiak and Monique (Dad's Boston Bull Terrier and life partner since Mom died) both danced playfully on the beach knowing something great just happened.

Too bad Kelsey wasn't here to witness this incredible family moment. She was perched high above the lake on a rocky cliff immersed in a book that took her far away. It was as if some angel lifted her eyes from her book just in time to see her granddad charging by on a jet ski! The girl with the magnificent eyes was treated to a magnificent sight.

And what about me, the one-time cheerleader? I was back in my element (add 40-plus years and 50-plus pounds) cheering those fellas on to heroic victory!! Some things never die.

And yet, they do. But the memories and the moments of such compelling joy will live on forever in the minds of those of us fortunate enough to have experienced them. Just like this stunning sunrise that Kodiak and I now share, our sunset shall be equally beautiful. And then, there will be yet another sunrise to illuminate the true treasures in our lives.

– Dianne Hough
Real Estate Top Producer
Mother of Two
Boise, Idaho
dianne@spro.net

Nobody Who Rides a New York Subway Has Anything on Me!

Rich Hallstrom

At some point along the way, people ask their own version of the question, "What is the purpose for my life?" I asked myself that question approximately six years ago. My search for the answer opened the door for me to discover the essence of who I am, forever changing the way I view myself and live my life.

My life has been filled with challenges. I was born with Spastic Diplegia, a form of Cerebral Palsy that causes a disability that affects my motor skills and coordination. While each of us has unique challenges and circumstances that are beyond our control, I have come to see that how I respond to those challenges is what makes the difference for me. I choose to focus on what I *can do* rather than on my limitations, an attitude that has taken some time to develop.

One such opportunity came at age eight when I experienced one of the saddest days in my life. It was an ordinary day in Seattle when my mom told me I would never play football, a reminder that I was not a 'normal' guy. Or was I?

The overcast weather that day seemed to settle in my soul. What I could not yet envision was how my passion for the game and my unique talents would allow me to 'play' in a different way than I had imagined. As a kid, I began to create my own sports casts and broadcast them through the microphone of a small stereo during game time. I loved sports and my knowledge level wasn't far behind the fulltime announcers. I taught myself how to write articles. I began to slowly realize that my limitations could actually open doors of opportunity. Imagine how our lives would change if we lived that truth every day!

I eventually became a Sports Columnist for the Issaquah Press during high school. I never played football, but I did make it to the NFL as a reporter for *Seahawks Saturday*.

Those early years held many reminders that I wasn't exactly like everyone else, and I mistakenly took that to mean that I was inferior in some way. I had trouble seeing my value. Despite many successes (my marriage, an exciting job, and good friends), I still felt a void until I began to see myself as God intended, a whole, unique man gifted for a specific purpose.

My key mistake up until this point in life was consulting everyone and everything except God, the One who knew me best of all. I heard that if you want to learn about a work of art you must consult the artist. I chose to believe that I was one of His masterpieces, so I opened my mind and heart to all He had for me … and the understanding, contentment and the new beginnings began to fill my life immediately. I have learned to live by the message of Ephesians 2:10, "For we are God's workmanship, created in Jesus Christ to do good works..." I needed to stop questioning and start living!

Today, I am a freelance sports reporter. It is my responsibility to find, develop, and sell stories to various media outlets. I love the challenges associated with my line of work. Living well with my disability has enhanced my skills as a freelance reporter. It has given me the ability to develop focus, persistence, a competitive edge, and an ability to see a unique story in every person. I have been privileged to interview some of sport's elite such as Steve Young, Michael Jordan, and even Dennis Rodman. My sixteen year history as an integral part of the Seattle Seahawks press team has afforded me some awesome experiences and has gained me the respect of the athletes and coaches alike. I enjoy friendships with Coach Mike Holmgren, the coaching staff, and many Seahawks players. I play a valued role and have a positive impact on the team. It reminds me that anyone can accomplish tremendous things when they set their hearts and minds to it.

Since I use a wheelchair for mobility, even the process of simply showing up for work is challenging for me. Perseverance has become a great companion in my life. It takes me two bus rides and a long arduous 'push' through the rowdy crowd to finally make it to the press box on game day at Qwest Field. The agility that it takes to maneuver this chair through the crowd surely requires the skill of an athlete. **Nobody who rides a New York Subway has anything on me!**

The close of the game leads me on another adventure as I head down to the locker room for interviews. Wedging a wheelchair into the ideal spot to get an interview with the key players of the day can be a bit demanding, but well worth the effort. That is a great life lesson ... the worthwhile things in life often require a bit of effort and perseverance.

Today, I continue my work with the Seahawks. I also have had my own segment on their official show. I believe the impact is high when people see me talking about football from my wheelchair. My message focuses on pursuing your passions with excellence. No disability, challenge or life circumstance can stand in the way unless you allow it to.

The circumstances in my life aren't an idealistic theory but an objective reality. God opened the doors for me to experience a trip to Athens to attend the XXII Paralympic Games as a member of the broadcast team for 2KPlus Sports Media International. Significant work, international travel, and a life full of purpose. God has honored me. He longs to do the same for you. Open your heart to the possibilities, pursue your passions, recognize your unique value and live a life of gratitude and service. Stop questioning and start living! **If you remember anything I have written on these pages, let it be that your life and what you are created to do and be truly has an extraordinary purpose.**

– *Rich Hallstrom*
Director, Motivation with a Purpose
Motivational Speaker
Sports Broadcast Professional
crichh@aol.com

"So Much Is So Good"

Mildred Stewart

"For truly as you have come, I have called you.
Come from the perplexities. Come from the busyness
… Be a fountain pouring forth joy and life and
love as you wait and as you serve."

– A passage from *Come and Rest* by Mildred Stewart

This morning my friend called. We had only greeted one another when I shared one of my favorite sayings: "So much is so good!" She quickly replied, "That is the first line of your story." And so it is.

There is so much that is so good! Let me count the ways. I was born into a Christian home. We were taught not to lie … I remember two lies I told as a child which made quite an impression. We were also not allowed to swear, so our slang words were 'my land', 'holy cow' and 'good grief'. Our family was built upon the foundational values that made our nation great.

My grandparents came West in 1868, along with other settlers. They lived in a one room dwelling with a lean-to as they joined with the community to build a house of worship. Serving God was their highest priority. They met in homes while the church was being built, solid evidence that the church is committed individuals, not merely a building. My grandfather dug a 15' by 22' by 8' deep hole for our home basement using only a simple spade. The original structure now has additional rooms with modern amenities. But originally, we relied on wood heat year round.

We lived off of the farm in every sense, growing and harvesting our own fruits and vegetables, grinding our own flour, and raising livestock. Our clothing was made by hand and we traveled by horse and buggy until 1917.

I watched as cars, airplanes and farm machinery were developed. I also watched in amazement as telephone, radio, TV and computers were invented. Computers ... turning the world into a different place that I often fail to recognize.

Along with great gain came some sense of loss, as times of quiet were being pushed aside. With the old way of life, there was always an unimaginable amount of work to do at home and on the farm ... but we had our space and our quiet times. How grateful I am for modern conveniences, yet how I long for many aspects of that life, especially for the type of schools I experienced as a student and later as a teacher myself. I am also saddened by the changing priorities of our nation, as God has become someone that most seem to have little time for. I pray for everyone to realize that a life without God is worthless, regardless of the comforts and successes you may enjoy in this modern world.

We three children studied around the kitchen table, learning disciplined study skills that served us as we worked our way through college during the time of The Great Depression. My mother wrote in 1935, "Next week Daddy will sell a rooster, and I will send you a dollar."

Despite the challenges, we each succeeded in our professions, married and raised our families. As children, we had all lived in one community where family was a big part of our lives. After World War II, everyone was separated from coast to coast.

We had grown up running barefoot over the land roamed by Native Americans only a couple of decades before our grandparents came. Yet, we were changing as a nation with our moral fiber weakening and our commitment to our neighbor eroding. The faster pace of this new life threatened to steal those quiet times.

Now I've passed the fourscore years of my life, and as I write my family history, I find my purpose more meaningful than ever! I live a rewarding life. I love being near many of my children, grandchildren, and even great grandchildren. I often enjoy journaling in my quiet times. I have become a counselor in my apartment community. I drive and do my own errands. My church, a true lifeline, is just four blocks away. My life is filled with great friends. My life is filled with blessing after blessing. God has lovingly cared for my family all these years. I am grateful to be protected by His hand.

While my book of life is full of good memories, life still changes. In fact, I often feel that I'm the only one left. I've much to do yet. As I cherish my children and grandchildren, I pray for each by name every day.

Quoting from my book of my family's life story, "I believe perhaps the greatest legacy one can give is to know what one believes – and what is the foundation of that believing." I fully believe that those answers are found in God's Word. May it become the "bottom line" of your living, the source of your joy and strength. May you, truly find your life filled with, "So much that is so good."

– Mildred Stewart
Wife, Mother, Grandmother
Age 87
Tulsa, Oklahoma

Signal Your Intention, Not Your Turn

Gaye Lindfors

Are you on a life journey that has a clear destination? Do you have a roadmap that will get
you there with joy-filled focus? Do you begin each
day knowing that you are living intentionally,
using your talents and gifts on work and activities
that you embrace passionately?

Before you let your giggles or cynicism get the
best of you, just think about it. We are meant to
live this way! I recognize that some of you may be
thinking, "Get real, lady! Wake up and smell the
coffee!" But others may recognize a little stirring in
your soul that says, *"That's what I really want!"*

A basic principle used while driving a car can be
applied to our lives. When we get in the driver's
seat, we have a destination in mind. We are going
somewhere with purpose. To make sure we end up

at the right place, we follow directions. By following the directions, we know when it is time to turn to the left or to the right. And before we turn, we put on our turn signal. Because we know in advance where we are going, we signal our intention to turn, not just at the last minute. Apply that to life: we have a clear destination (our purpose), we create a roadmap for getting there (our plan), and then we make the turns - choices and decisions – deliberately. (We follow our plan!) This is living intentionally. *It all begins with knowing why you are here and where you are going.*

It took me a number of years to discover that living with purpose was not the same as being successful. Like many of my colleagues and friends, my title, perks, salary, and location of my box on the organization chart defined success. By those definitions, I was doing quite well. I was director of human resources for an international Fortune 500 company advising a business unit of 11,000 employees. But my heart longed to do something else. I didn't know what that "something else" was; I just knew I needed a reason for living that was bigger than my current life.

And so my "journey of purpose" began. Countless hours were spent studying, praying, reading, and engaging my friends and family in discussions on mission and vision, calling, and intentional living.

My purpose eventually became clear. I was created to highlight, celebrate, and inspire *significance* in others and myself. This is my calling. This is how I will leave my mark on the world.

Meanwhile, the disenchantment with my corporate position increased and I found myself asking God – sometimes begging God – to just open the door and allow me to walk away from it all. But for two years His answer was a clear 'no' until one Friday morning in early September 2002. While listening to a discussion during a senior leadership team meeting, I realized that there was very little conversation that was inspiring a sense of significance for any of us! That wasn't a criticism of the team; it's just that the difference between the corporation's purpose and my purpose had become clear. I heard myself softly whisper under my breath, "It's time to go." I immediately felt at peace. God's timing had come. Seven weeks later, I was a joy-filled, re-energized, unemployed, middle-aged woman who began living the life she was meant to live.

I have my own consulting business now. The contentment experienced through my work is extraordinary. Every day my clients and audiences allow me to use my expertise and experience to create a better tomorrow and to remind them in subtle and not-so-subtle ways, that they are significant. Together, we find business and life solutions that are built on the foundation of purpose...excellence…significance. I have opened the gift of living with purpose.

An Almighty God created you for a purpose that no one else can fulfill. You are an amazing person with gifts, abilities, characteristics, warts, and pimples. When you leave this earth, no one can replace you. No one else can ever be you. That makes you significant. And that is why it is so important that you live with purpose.

You are in the driver's seat. You can ignore any map, take the turns that seem correct at the last minute, and be surprised where you end up. Or you can follow your directions, turn intentionally, and pull up to the curb of your planned destination.

All of us are going somewhere in life…choose to go somewhere with purpose.

– Gaye Lindfors
Business Consultant, Professional Speaker
Significant Solutions, Inc.
651-490-9550
glindfors@comcast.net
www.significantsolutionsinc.com

I've begun to think of myself as wealthy because I realize that I carry within myself most of what I need to make me happy.

~ Cathleen Roundtree

Recognize Your
True Wealth

Today's Special: Life! ... Served With Emotion and Effort

Sara Seed

You are sitting at your favorite restaurant. You know the one they recognize your voice when you make a reservation; seat you at your favorite table without hesitation; remember that you like seventeen creams in your coffee and bring them without making fun of you, (at least not to your face). Then, without warning, they've changed the daily specials without your permission! How could they? Yet, as you read through the new menu, you discover specials you never could have imagined! Instantly, you realize that sometimes, when you let go of your expectations, amazing, really wonderful things can happen.

This scenario is a lot like life. Just when you think you have it all figured out, something happens – good or bad – that makes you re-adjust your priorities and even appreciate the unknown. Another example: I was put into left field in the last inning of a softball game between my team, the ferocious Kittens and our opponents, the mighty Chix. I was only eight, so playing was rare but I was always ready. I would show up early, wear my glove the entire game and give my coach that pitiful "put me in please look" which I had practiced in the mirror, yet the game would usually end with me on the bench. But this night was different.

When the coach barked my name I sprinted into left field and assumed my position. One out, two outs... and no action, other than swatting mosquitoes and contemplating my concession stand order. Then, whack! The ball flew off the bat and was headed right towards me! I tracked that ball, shut my eyes and waited for it to smack me on the head. When I looked in my glove, to everyone's surprise (including mine), there it was! I held that ball up like the Olympic torch! The crowd went wild...all twenty of them! I never could have known ahead of time that this amazing moment would be a turning point. I learned that if I worked hard enough, I could be something special.

As an athlete, I was coached never to let the opponent see my feelings. It was a sign of weakness if they sensed any kind of emotion, so I always kept mine in check. I translated that lesson from sports into my personal life. I was twenty-one the first time I publicly wept. My college coach was killed in a car accident. I never knew I could shed so many tears, and for once, I didn't care who saw me. The loss was just unbearable. Yet, allowing myself to grieve her loss taught me I was not weak for showing emotion. It just meant I was human. Life presents circumstances that are full of emotion and drama. This lesson continues to mold me as an educator, businesswoman and speaker to this day.

Our society focuses almost single-mindedly on outcome and not nearly enough on the effort made in the process. Several years ago, I came face to face with the valuable lessons offered by others' efforts. I was scheduled for my fourth back surgery in three years. My entire community came forward. Friends called, sent cards and prepared enough food for ten family reunions! I tried to act strong but I was scared to death. The day before we left for Mayo Clinic, friends from our church came to our home and presented me with a list of church members who were scheduled to pray for me on the day of surgery. The list was broken down into fourteen hours with ten-minute shifts...and it was full. My family and I were overwhelmed by this gesture of support. Some slots were doubled up.

On the day of surgery, the doctors were behind schedule. I kept asking my parents what time it was and a nurse finally asked why I was so concerned. I replied, "I have people praying for me and if we don't hurry, those prayers will end before my surgery begins!" Overwhelmed with emotion, Mom took my hand and said, "Sara, I don't think God wears a watch."

I had it all wrong. It wasn't about the outcome. It was about the effort. What do I mean by effort? Effort is my mother, who rivals Shirley McClain in "Terms of Endearment," cornering the nurses and insisting on getting me pain medicine. Effort is my father quietly delivering turkeys to unassuming families in need the night before Thanksgiving. And on September 11th, the operator who made the effort to stay on the phone with Todd Beamer and calmly guided him from one life into the next. Outcomes may be unpredictable and are often unfathomable; they can be surprisingly wonderful or completely devastating. But it's the emotion and effort that compliment the "special" of the day which guides us back to our lives...and ultimately, back to ourselves.

– Sara Seed
President of Sara Seed Promotions, llc
Professional Speaker, Event Specialist
217-403-9999
sspromo@soltec.net
www.saraseedpromotions.com

Julia

Kathy Pride

It was such a long time ago...over 25 years. But what choice did I have? I was young, in college, and I saw no way out. I pretended it was an easy decision. I convinced myself there was no other choice. The people at the clinic presented a clinical and impersonal description of the options and made a required, but feeble attempt to present them all. Their bias was very clear, and at the time, reassuring. After all, it upheld my decision.

The tiny life already established in my womb was referred to as "products of conception." The life-giving option of adoption was one I dismissed as too difficult. How could I give my child away? I thought it was easier to snuff out a life. I was a freshman at an Ivy League College and I had so much to lose. The choice was automatic. Have an abortion and forget about it. Get on with life.

At first I was defiant in justifying the decision I had made. It was the late 70's. It was my right to manage my body. Women everywhere told me so. The clump of cells growing inside me was part of my body, not a separate and unique life. But in time, the horror of a discarded life started to smolder inside me, burning a hole, a deep abyss of emptiness inside my heart and soul.

Every June, when the baby that never was – whom I later named Julia – would have been born, I noticed children who would be her age and would ask myself a hundred unanswerable questions. What would she have looked like? Would she have had dark hair like me? Would she have dressed in bows and frills, parading around in party shoes, or would she have been a tomboy, swinging upside down from tree branches and clamoring with abandon on the jungle gym? Would she have loved me? I loved her...

The years passed and I buried milestones of her unlived life deep inside me. Off to kindergarten ... a toothless grin ... elementary school ... piano recitals ... junior high ... the prom ... graduation ... college ... and perhaps by now married and a mother herself. But I was ashamed...so ashamed. And the burden of shame grew heavier and heavier. It was like a rock too heavy to carry. And, oh, how I tried to cast it off! I tried to prevent the secret from consuming me, but denial, justification, shame, guilt, and self-condemnation encased me like a cocoon, holding me captive.

Three years after my abortion, I married a wonderful man I met in college and settled into a normal life. We started our family right away and had two sons within three years. The following years were busy as my husband completed medical school and I worked with expectant families as a childbirth educator. When my husband finished his residency training, we decided we wanted another child, and I assumed I would get pregnant right away. But we were dealt a hand of secondary infertility and pregnancy loss. My work as a childbirth educator seemed like a cruel joke. I was certain my miscarriage and infertility were punishment from God for the abortion I had had. And then, five years after embarking on the journey of infertility, we brought home our daughter from Vietnam who shared her birthday with the anniversary of Julia's death. And then, two years later, I found myself pregnant with our youngest daughter.

Twenty-four years had elapsed since that blustery November day when I had given up my first child. By this time I was a mother of four, and my marriage of 21 years was faltering under the pressure of many stresses. Our oldest son, now a sophomore in college, was struggling academically. Our second son found himself in drug rehab, gripped by the addiction to marijuana. The girls were young and demanding. My life was far from the normal one I craved.

A storm of chaos raged in my life over which I felt I had no control. I had nowhere to look, but towards heaven. I collapsed into the arms of a loving and patient God who had been calling my name for years.

I heard God's voice when I was invited to a local pregnancy care center. It was there that I learned more about the healing work offered for people like me suffering from post-abortive stress syndrome. I knew the anguish I felt was real. I just didn't know it was a recognized disorder. I never expected that a Christian organization would respond to my pain with love and support. Because of their loving spirit, I learned about a merciful and gracious God, who had abounding love for me, could heal me, and also use my experience to provide healing and comfort to others. And it was then that I realized that God had forgiven me, and had cast away my transgressions, *"As far as the east is from the west."* (Psalm 103:11-12.)

In my heart, I knew God had forgiven me, but a battle continued to rage inside me. Could I forgive myself? I grappled with the feeling that somehow I was betraying Julia's memory if I forgave myself. I struggled with the difference between forgiving and forgetting. I knew I would never forget, but I also knew I had to forgive myself and discard the cloak of shame I had worn for so many years in order for God to use me to help others.

God has shown me in a real way that He has forgiven me. He gave me a daughter, born to another woman in a country halfway around the world on the same November date that so many years before I had made an unforgettable, yet forgivable decision. God also ensured Julia's memory in the heart of her father. I found out that he also has a daughter born on that same November date. And I have a peace that someday I will be able to see my Julia for the first time and ask for her forgiveness.

For many years, I couldn't understand the purpose of my experiences: crisis pregnancy, pregnancy loss, and becoming an adoptive mother. But these experiences have helped shape me into who I am today, and they have allowed me to see the evidences of God's grace and forgiveness through the intersection of one date and three unique, yet connected children's lives. I have grieved and let go of the shame. And for this I am grateful for a forgiving and merciful God.

– Kathy Pride
Author/Speaker
Tapestry Ministries: Weaving Lives of New Possibility
570-271-0192
Kathy@Tapestryministry.com
www.tapestryministry.com

Big Impact

Brandi Swindell

In the summer of 1997, I was working on staff in Yellowstone Park. During that time, one of my roommates became pregnant and decided to have an abortion. I prayed, pleaded and counseled her that she not move forward with this decision. In spite of all these efforts, she had the abortion. That decision changed her and my life forever.

At first I was struck by the hypocrisy of our society. Here, in Yellowstone Park, one was not even allowed to pick flowers or disturb the beauty of God's creation. In fact, you could be arrested and fined if you were caught violating any of the park's regulations concerning destroying the natural habitat. Yet, my roommate, with full protection of the law could destroy the most beautiful of all God's creation...an innocent child. I was shocked and stunned that America's greatest natural treasure, unborn children, had no legal protection at all.

I saw firsthand the pain and trauma a woman experiences when she has an abortion. My room-mate was not "liberated" by the experience of abortion. In fact, she was broken and devastated. Her life and self-esteem were scarred. I wept not only for her but also for all the millions of women who were wounded by abortion and living in silent prisons of guilt and shame.

At that moment, I knew I must do something. How could I be silent while this horrific loss of innocent human life was taking place around me? How could I do nothing while women my age were being exploited and violated by abortion? I cried out to God to stir my heart and use me as an instrument of His healing and love. I also prayed for God to use me as a voice to provoke the conscience of the church.

Little did I realize the impact of that prayer on my life. It is hard to believe that seven years later, God has answered it in an extraordinary fashion. He has led in a way that I could have never planned or orchestrated. It has been nearly impossible for me to comprehend that I would co-found Generation Life, a national pro-life ministry. Or, that I would travel across the nation as well as in other countries sharing the gospel of Christ and the message of life with thousands of people. And, I would have never even thought of being asked to appear on national TV and radio shows or featured in national newspapers. I could not have fathomed having the opportunity to organize events in front of the White House and United States Capitol.

The goal of my ministry, Generation Life, is to reach out and build a culture of life for this generation. Each person can find a place to build the culture of life and share the pro-life message. For the staff and volunteers of Generation Life, we like to use the phrase "Now it's our turn to make history!" That means it is our responsibility to stand up with passion and courage and proclaim the gospel of life.

The words of the Rev. Martin Luther King Jr., from a Birmingham jail cell 40 years ago, speak to us powerfully today with respect to abortion. "There was a time when the church was very powerful. It was during that period when the early Christians rejoiced when they were deemed worthy to suffer for what they believed. In those days, the church was not merely a thermometer that recorded the ideas and principles of popular opinion, it was a thermostat that transformed...society."

My purpose in life is to empower people to reflect God's heart and be the practical application of His compassion. Think of how the heart of God must be aching for the 47 million children whose lives were so prematurely taken through abortion. These children will never laugh, see the beauty of a sunrise, or feel the warm embrace of a loving parent. Could it be, that lost in the past 32 years since abortion was legalized, was a researcher who would have found the cure for cancer? Or, a surgeon who might have discovered new operating procedures that would have saved thousands of lives?

God does not grieve only for the children. His heart also aches for the millions of women whose lives have been crushed by abortion; women who feel the guilt and shame of their actions every day but are alone, trapped and afraid. We must minister forgiveness and grace in our hearts or women will never feel free to come forward for healing.

The Christian community can be the place that provides a loving and affirming atmosphere for women seeking help and wholeness. The church must boldly proclaim there is no sin too great to separate one from the love of Christ or the love of His children. My church, the Vineyard Boise has started a life-affirming ministry that helps women work through the pain of abortion and achieve spiritual and emotional wholeness.

It is my prayer that those who seek to live their lives with purpose will bring an end to abortion. If a young single woman in Yellowstone could stand alone for life, then you can find purpose in restoring a generation of life. My challenge to you is to be the one person that begins making a difference in this struggle we all face for life.

– Brandi Swindell
National Director, Generation Life
208-867-1307
www.generationlife.net

Living Beyond Grief

Suzi Boyle

My father was an Air Force dad who was also a writer/cartoonist from Gloucester, Massachusetts. He was a blonde haired blue eyed, good Catholic altar boy. My mother was a pure blood Samurai from Japan, a Buddhist with very regal roots. For religious and socio-economic reasons, they were both disowned by their families for marrying. My first bed was a Dole banana box at the time when the three of us were dropped off in Seattle, Washington, with no money, no relatives and no support system.

Dad was eventually hired as a newspaper editor in the small town of Payette, Idaho, and a train ride brought us to this new home in the middle of nowhere. I always knew, even though we grew up in a rural agricultural town, that we didn't quite fit into that stereotype. Having both Eastern and Western influences, I was raised to be goal-directed and ambitious, while simultaneously modest and not boastful. While I have achieved many awards and accolades in my career thus far, I always remember the teachings of my parents: the importance of humility and self-sacrifice.

I went through a turbulent divorce when I was thirty-one after eleven years of marriage. The most positive outcome of my marriage was my wonderful son, Jonathan, who, at the time, was only in kindergarten. I took my dad's advice and chose to walk away from a decade of hard work building a successful real estate company with my husband in order to save my integrity, health, dignity, and, most of all, in hopes of raising my child in a much healthier environment. My father was correct when he said that you can always re-create money but it is very difficult to restore the aforementioned qualities when they are lost. This advice turned out to be a gentle and effective pathway to my empowerment that enabled me to recover from the pain of divorce. Since that time, I have used my experiences during that trial to empower literally hundreds of other divorcing women on many levels: emotional, physical, financial, and legal.

Soon after my divorce I began praying to the Lord; "Please let me only fall in love one more time. I cannot go through the pain again." It wasn't very long before God sent the right man for me – my true soul mate. Being wary and skeptical that this could happen within only a few months, we made the decision to have a long engagement: five years! We've been together for thirteen years and have had a wonderful marriage with many periods of growth. We just recently helped our son move to San Diego to attend his dream college. Along the way we've had life's typical bumps and elations. We are proud to have come through these with a positive attitude...the glass is half-full in our lives, not half-empty.

The biggest challenge along the way has been the untimely and violent homicides of both my parents in 1998. My mother assisted a young woman out of an abusive marriage and when the husband discovered this, he stalked and then murdered my mother with her own kitchen butcher knife. My father walked in on the struggle, and was also murdered. This event not only challenged every bit of faith I ever had in God, but also in the judicial system, as the jury acquitted the murderer. I constantly asked God and myself, "Why are we still here while they are gone?" In the beginning, my maternal drive kept me alive. I wanted life to stay as normal as possible for their only grandchild, my son.

Eventually, I had to succumb to the roller coaster of the emotion that is grief. A decision that I made very early in the grief process ended up preserving my sanity and kept my family intact. I refused to remember my parents by what happened on the last day they were here on earth, but rather chose to revere them for all the unbelievable acts of love and good they contributed to humankind in their sixty-eight years on this earth. Consequently, my family has given multiple memorials and dedications in their memory, in print, cement and real estate, to continue their legacy of community service. My hope is that this will be a lasting legacy for many future generations. My prayer is that it will inspire those who knew my parents – especially Jonathan.

My parents themselves embodied the philosophy that they espoused to my siblings and me. They lived spectacular lives yet never acted like it. They contributed to their community in countless ways. They made innumerable sacrifices to do what was right for their family, including putting their careers on hold at times, and even choosing to give birth to me when they had once considered abortion. Ever mindful of their many sacrifices, I strive to live the way they did: to give all I can to other people and to leave this place a little bit better than I found it.

– Suzi Boyle
Mortgage Banker
208-947-3355
sboyle@youngmortgage.com
www.suziboyle.com

Powerlessness Equals Power

Doreen Bessette Sicotte

It was a beautiful spring day in 1995, and as was my routine, it was time for my annual physical. I was 55 years old, and taking care of myself was and still is very important to me. On this visit, as I had the year before, I complained to my doctor that my right ear seemed to be plugged, and I was having difficulty hearing. After checking and finding no blockage, my doctor referred me to a hearing specialist. I was given many different tests, the last of which was a CAT scan where they discovered a benign brain tumor the size of an egg yolk on the right hearing and facial nerve. I learned that this potentially fatal tumor was called an acoustic neuroma.

The doctors assured me that while the tumor was an issue, the surgery was not a life-threatening situation. The removal procedure would mean that the right hearing nerve would have to be severed, leaving me deaf in that ear, but that my left ear would still be functional. Their main concern was saving the facial nerve. If they could not manage to save it, the right side of my face would be paralyzed and I would be disfigured for life. I agreed to the surgery and was put on a waiting list in a hospital six hours away from my home in Kelowna, British Columbia.

When I received this prognosis, I was deeply involved with the study of Science of Mind that teaches that we create our own life experiences with our beliefs. I could not reconcile this teaching with what I was experiencing. Did I actually want this and create this? If I created this tumor, how could I prevent others? Did I really have this much power within?

In late August 1995, after celebrating our daughter Gina and Nick's wedding in Regina, Saskatchewan, I found myself anxious and unsettled. I decided that I needed some solitude to come to terms with what was happening to me. I made reservations at a local retreat house to contemplate my situation and restore my wounded spirit. I remember having two books with me, 'The Thunder of Silence' by Joel S. Goldsmith and 'A Course in Miracles'. During those four days by myself, I walked, I cried, I slept, I read, I prayed, I meditated and I had a vivid dream of being comforted by my parents. My greatest fear was making it through the operation only to awake different in my mind, my spirit, and my body. I felt powerless.

It was during this time that I began to look within. I began to understand that the powerlessness I felt was my feeble human spirit, and I discovered that also within me was an untapped resource of strength and power and wisdom found in my divine spirit. God became my strength and hope. I opened myself up to learn what it meant to have a complete reliance on my own inner, higher power.

When the call came in the fall of that year, I was powerful. My husband and love of my life for 35 years, Bert, and my daughters, Colette, Linda, and Gina, all traveled great distances across Canada to be with me. I was so grateful and honored to have them all there. I felt loved, cared for and cherished.

On October 19, 1995, two caring and competent doctors, Dr. Griesdale and Dr. Noel performed my operation. The operation lasted eight hours. When I finally awoke, my first image was of Dr. Griesdale looking at me from about 3 inches away from my face. What a blessing! He quickly reassured me that the operation had gone very well, there was no brain damage, and they were successful in saving the facial nerve. The gratitude, the joy and the relief I felt, and am still feeling today, cannot be described in words. This experience changed the way I deal with everything in my life. For I now know that there is power in a complete surrender to the Divine.

– Doreen Bessette Sicotte
Ordained Minister
The International Alliance of
the Churches of Truth, Canada
250-769-6480
doreen.sicotte@shaw.ca

Get in the Game

Jodee Bock

I heard on the radio today that someone in my neighboring state of Minnesota became a millionaire overnight when he won the state lottery. Yeah, but winning the lottery only happens to other people, right?

What if it could happen to you? Well, guess what ... it actually *could* happen to you. I know, because it happened to me.

OK, it's not the lottery you're thinking of. I'm no millionaire. I've never won an Olympic medal. I'm not a doctor or a lawyer or a CEO. But I struck it rich when I stumbled upon the notion of doing things on purpose.

Stumbling across an insight can happen to anyone. How many times have you been walking along and all of a sudden, out of nowhere, for no apparent reason, you trip? You first look around to see if anyone else saw you, and you might glance down to see what you tripped over, but usually you want to move on as quickly as possible and forget that it ever happened (especially if there were witnesses!).

But it's when we become intentional about those stumbles that real results start to show up. When we get to the point of actually noticing what grabs our attention – and then moving beyond the *noticing* to the *doing* – we'll be living our lives on purpose.

There's a coffee shop across the street from my office. Even though it's a franchise, it has the feel of a unique specialty shop all because of Nancy, the gal who runs the place. Because of Nancy, every employee at this coffee shop knows the customers by name and makes them feel like family. I've been noticing what makes Nancy and her shop stand out for quite a while, but I had never really *done* anything with that noticing until yesterday.

Yesterday I felt compelled to tell Nancy that I noticed that she really values her customers *and* her employees – and I know they notice it, too. She said she loves her job and business is great, but she's at the point that she needs to decide how to handle it without working even more hours than she already does. I told her to listen to her head brain, but to make sure her heart brain and her gut brain were in line, too, and she would just know what was right for her. She looked me in the eye and said, "thank you so much for that coaching." I knew that she appreciated the greatness I not only saw in her, but mentioned to her – on purpose.

Being intentional and doing things on purpose – even if at first you stumble – has powerful effects in the world. Since I learned about the power of intention, I've also become aware that the words I choose impact the outcomes I get in my life. Some words come with their own baggage – their own implied context. But I have the power to use different words to create new contexts. Those items on my personal schedule I used to think of as *obligations* somehow lost their oppressiveness when I started thinking of them as *responsibilities* – and even gained power when I called them *opportunities*.

Even the word **POWER** might have its own baggage, especially if it's been used in contexts that imply force or control. The way I choose to think of my personal power is by the acronym **P**urpose, **O**pen-mindedness, **W**isdom, **E**nergy, **R**esponsibility. What a new context the word POWER now has for me!

Have you ever gone to a movie on opening night? Chances are pretty good that unless you get there very early, you will be standing in line. If you become frustrated at the long wait and leave the line, only to get to your car and decide you really do want to see the movie, you'll find yourself much further behind than if you'd just stayed where you were once you rejoin the line.

I've found myself frustrated at my place in line in my life, but didn't realize until later that if I'd kept my feet pointed toward the goal, I could have allowed myself to turn my head around and see how far I'd come, which would have encouraged me to stay on the path without losing ground.

There is POWER in not turning back, and giving yourself credit for where you are. What keeps you from acting on your insights? Be careful not to allow the agenda of others to cause you to abandon what your head, heart and gut are telling you. You can never really know when the little thing you say or the loving look you give someone when you're acting on purpose might be the moment that changes someone's life. It cost me nothing to share my thoughts with Nancy, but the value of her smile and sincerity were worth more to me than that winning lottery ticket.

As we become more intentional about growing who we long to be, what we do will naturally follow. Like winning the lottery, being intentional and living life on purpose – with purpose – really can happen to anyone. But, also like the lottery, you can't win if you're not in the game. So make today the day you choose to get in the game and celebrate your worthwhile purpose of living intentionally.

And next time you stumble, notice what you

notice on the way down. Take a minute to intentionally examine what it was that tripped you up. It might just be a jackpot in disguise.

– Jodee Bock
Partner, One Degree
jodee@onedeg.com
www.onedeg.com

*Doing your best at this moment
puts you in the best place for
the next moment.*

~ Oprah Winfrey

Giving Your Best Today
Insures Your Best Tomorrow

Finding Your Family Vision

David Barrett

A family of purpose can turn the sorrows of yesterday into the joys of tomorrow. It is not difficult to realize that there is a significant amount of havoc in many families today. We see this in divorce, rebellious teen-agers, child abuse, parent abuse and many other difficulties that families are facing. It is possible that you or someone close to you is living in these difficult situations right now. What was, and even what is, does not have to be that way forever. Just because you have a broken or dysfunctional family situation now or in the past, doesn't mean that this has to be a reoccurring cycle.

The wisdom found in the Bible and a life committed to a purpose greater than yourself makes it possible to establish a family that lives with purpose. This solidifies the impact of the family as the stabilizing unit in society. A family with purpose creates a ripple effect, one where each family member is impacted and the impact extends to those outside that family. God designed the family to be a blessing. We are reminded of the joy of families being together in Proverbs 17:6, "Children's children are the crown of old men; and the glory of children are their fathers."

I believe that our culture has lost true family vision. Families often don't have a purpose that they seek to follow and fulfill. Does your family have a vision? Would you like to see more joy and blessing in your family? You can.

When I first got married, I knew nothing about purposeful family living. Though raised in a Christian home and desiring to please God, I had no thought of having or establishing a family vision. When my wife and I married, though we held the Godly standards of faithfulness to each other, we married for very selfish reasons. We married because we liked being loved and cared for, besides we were at the right age where everyone gets married. There was little talk of children and family, only that we wanted to have some, some day.

Looking back, I see that we were headed for destruction if I had not been sensitive to what the Lord wanted to teach me.

Immediately after we married, we traveled clear to the other side of the country for me to attend graduate school. There I was supported by my wife to fulfill my vision, but together we had little more than just the appearance of "family potential". If my wife hadn't been completely dedicated to see us through these rough first years, and I hadn't discovered God's view of the family, we would have sunk in the sea of married life without purpose.

What made the difference? I read the words of a wise, elderly gentleman who had pondered God's purpose for the family and unselfishly shared his insights. The following words struck a chord in my heart and mind.

"It needs more than ever to be stressed that the best and truest educators are parents under God. The greatest school is the family. In learning, no act of teaching in any school or university compares to the routine task of mothers in teaching a babe who speaks no language. No other task in education is equal to this. The moral training of the child, the discipline of good habits, is an inheritance from the parents to the child which surpasses all other. The family is the first and basic school of man." (R. J. Rushdooney)

These words spoke volumes to me, as I hope and trust they do to you as well. **The family is the first school.** It is the training ground for the next generation. The family is where God preserves the knowledge of the Scriptures and the purpose of life through the diligent preparation provided by parents. In this light, other verses of Scripture began to stand out, such as Psalms 127:3-5, "Lo, children are a heritage of the Lord: and the fruit of the womb is his reward. As arrows are in the hand of a mighty man; so are children of the youth. Happy is the man that hath his quiver full of them: they shall not be ashamed, but they shall speak with the enemies in the gate."

Can you sense the call of destiny in this verse? The family is far more than the place where a group of people, related by blood and marriage, co-exist and try to tolerate each other. The family is God's spiritual training center to raise children ready to change the culture!

From that moment, I was a man on a mission. It was not a mission by my self and for my self, but a mission with my wife, for our God and to our children. Our family purpose is not merely to survive and seek our own pleasures. We are committed to a destiny and an impact of generational proportions.

– David Barrett
Director, Biblical Worldview Learning Center
Administrator, Covenant Academy
Author, Speaker, Consultant
david@biblicalview.com
www.biblicalview.com

From Everglade City to Key West: The Adventure of Acceptance

Carl Drew

It all began with a book, a couple of beers, and a joke, the night before I was flying back home to Indiana. I shared the adventure story I was reading with my friend, Kurt. It was about a man who kayaked 120 miles through the Florida Everglades. He paddled through areas with names like: Alligator Creek, Hell's Bay, Shark River, and Graveyard Creek. I was 25 with an adventurous spirit, but my longest outdoor adventure to this point consisted of maybe a week of outdoor camping and 8 hours of kayaking. In jest, I threw out that maybe I could do something like him, and Kurt said he believed I could. That became the seed that grew into the adventure of a lifetime.

I cancelled my flight home and made reservations

to stay in South Florida for two months. I had no money and no experience. I didn't know a soul and I didn't even own a kayak, but I began planning a solo kayaking excursion that would be, not 120 miles, but 230 miles long. I didn't have a car, so I walked back and forth to the library to read everything I could about what I would need, how to prepare, the dangers to expect, and the bugs that were inevitable. Occasionally I would rent a bike and ride 40 miles round trip to the outfitter's to purchase the necessary equipment and maps.

The day finally came for me to begin my journey. Mentally I was ready, and I had all the supplies and equipment needed except one thing – a kayak! A friend drove me 100 miles to Everglade City where I found a shop by the Barron River. I purchased a used kayak from this little store that was going out of business that very day. As I put my kayak in the water, tourist and locals alike heckled me saying they would never even attempt this trip.

All along the way I watched as miracles unfolded before me. One evening as I was paddling toward camp with the sun setting on the horizon ahead, I was startled when two large dolphins jumped over the bow of my boat. They continued to play around me as I floated in awe wanting to capture the moment forever. A few days later I had a late start and found myself 5 miles from camp as dusk set in. I was faced with sleeping in my kayak when, for the first time in days I spotted a boat. Luckily, the couple aboard had been doing sponge research, and decided to anchor overnight. They invited me aboard and let me sleep on their deck. Near Flamingo, I met a gentleman kayaking. He gave me the phone number for his secretary who would help me with whatever I needed at the end of my journey including keys to his home and car, as well as all the food in his fridge.

But the journey was not to be without challenges. On one particular day, I was in the middle of the Florida Bay with no land in sight. The wind was fighting me horribly, and the waves were beating against me mercilessly. I couldn't take a break or the wind would push me back faster than I would coast forward. I remember fighting and becoming more angry with every stroke. Although no one was around, I shouted complaints about the futility of my efforts. I was about to snap when, with a wave of clarity, I realized I needed to let go of what I was expecting and enjoy what I was getting. I purposefully shifted my thinking to enjoying the wind, enjoying the splash of the water against me, and enjoying the experience even when it felt most difficult.

My worst day occurred about halfway through my trip to Flaming. I had read in one of the books about a shortcut, "The Nightmare", that would save me about 8.5 miles of paddling. All the books and maps warned that the tide had to be just right or I wouldn't make it through. I had some trepidation, but I figured this entire trip seemed to be about doing the impossible, so why not try.

The shortcut was about 2.5 miles long, and as I paddled the first 2 miles, I could see the water ebbing away as the tide was going out. The water was extremely mucky and I was constantly skidding over alligators with the bottom of my kayak. Downed trees and debris were exposed as the water level dropped. I had to get out quickly or I was going to be trapped or worse. I began paddling faster only to look up and see a tree ahead with a big red snake hanging down. Gripped with terror I nearly flipped the kayak into the gator-ridden waters to avoid the deadly snake!

Once again I found myself getting angry. What made me think I could paddle this river at half tide? Why didn't I listen to my Dad who said I was crazy to take such risks? Was I going to get out of this one alive? I soon realized that if I was going to survive, I needed to break free of the expectations and judgments, face the consequences of my decision, and create a new plan. I had to turn around and paddle my way back out of this nightmare. It was time to change my attitude and get to work on surviving.

It took me 21 days to complete my entire journey. A journey that I consider to be the best adventure of my life because of the life lessons I experienced. I learned that with knowledge, preparation, and faith in myself, I could do the impossible. I learned that anger doesn't come from the outside, but it comes from within. I learned that I had to accept responsibility for my decisions and the consequences that come with them. Best of all, I learned to let go of my expectations of what I think life should be like and simply enjoy what life is. Life is a beautiful, never-ending adventure!

– Carl Drew
Adventurer, Speaker, Filmmaker
260-438-6463
carl@carldrew.com
www.CarlDrew.com

The Roar of the Crowd

Maryanna Young

Through the course of my life, I have attended, played in and coached hundreds (maybe even thousands) of sporting events either as an athlete, coach or spectator. It would be impossible for me to recall the outcome of many of these events. Instead, I remember a few short segments from key events that have had a lasting impact on my life. One such instance occurred when I was watching a 10,000 meter race at the NCAA Track and Field Championships. It was an important race for the athletes involved, as it was the final race for many athletes that had trained for this moment since they were small children. The times would likely be near the best times in the world and those who finish well often go on to Olympic teams ... and win Olympic medals.

As a former competitor, I know that racing 10,000 meters on the track feels very long and grueling.

The race is just over 25 laps. It is not exactly the perfect spectator sport since the major excitement in the race comes down to the last couple of laps. Even at the elite levels, it takes the athletes around 30 minutes to finish. Many of the fans get bored well before that point and leave the stadium just before the excitement peaks. On the evening of this particular race, twenty thousand spectators were on the edge of their seats as this race took place. Several of the athletes involved were at the prime of their careers.

Just as the race began, a woman who was favored to win suddenly stepped to the side of the track and dropped to one knee. The crowd gasped and then groaned as they realized that this highly successful athlete had been stepped on by another athlete, causing her to lose her shoe. In the time it took her to replace and retie her track shoe, the other runners had raced ahead of her, leaving her at least a quarter of a lap behind the pack.

People in the stands began to talk about how unfortunate it was for such a great competitor to be out of a critical race due to circumstances beyond her control. Most of the crowd obviously expected her to walk off the track and chalk up her fate in the race to a disastrous mishap. How many of us make that same mistake when our circumstances overwhelm us and life feels beyond our control? All too often, we abandon what we were destined for in life. We give in to the circumstances that surround us.

What happened next is a scene that I will never forget...

The 21 year old, 105 pound athlete leaped to her feet and began to get back on pace to finish her remaining 25 laps. By now, she was an enormous distance from the back of the pack of runners. As she got back in the rhythm of running, it seemed unlikely that she would even finish the race. If she did finish, it appeared that she would be left out of award contention. The fans muttered about how dismal it was that this young woman's hard work had been completely wasted, and would cause her to finish short of where her potential might have taken her.

Each lap the fallen runner developed a faster rhythm to her stride. Miraculously, she was moving closer to the back of the pack of swiftly moving athletes. As a few more laps went by, it was clear that she was going to catch this group of the best collegiate runners in the world. As several more laps passed, the crowd moved their focus from the group of women leading the race. Nearly every eye was locked on the wiry young runner as she came from the back of the pack, inching her way closer to the leaders. Every person I could see began to rise to their feet and watch with amazement as this small, possibly injured athlete was making an unbelievable comeback. As each lap passed, the cheering crowd was louder than at any Super Bowl. Each person there seemed to get louder and louder as they began to share the mission of this unbelievable woman who wouldn't give in to her impossible situation. I am sure the women in the lead pack began to wonder why all the cheers were clearly behind them as they passed lap after lap. With four laps to go, the woman with the dream on her heart, vision in her mind and a crowd with deafening support was only 15 steps behind the leaders. The fans sensed she could not only make her way back to a respectable finish but she now had the potential to win.

Leigh Daniel did the impossible that day. She came from 100 meters behind and won the NCAA Championships to the deafening roar of the crowd.

This comeback is a powerful example of the amazing impact and results that come with encouragement. Simple applause began a flood of support that sparked hope in someone's heart. The result is often opportunity to achieve something far greater than we might on our own.

My purpose in life is to inspire people to be that encouraging force for those who are facing what seems like impossible circumstances in their everyday lives. I believe that there is a loving God that cheers for each of us regardless of our circumstances. Everyday, I learn so much from the clients that I coach and the young people that I mentor about what can be done to turn circumstances around and live daily with a vision for who they are destined to be.

Whose success and significance is depending on hearing your voice cheering them for who they are and what they can become? Is it your child or your co-worker, your clients or your friends, your spouse or your parents, that have lost sight of their dreams and their destiny? **Start the applause even when it might appear that all possibilities are gone and there is little or no hope.** Your personal enthusiasm and support can be the catalyst that changes the way that others see themselves.

– Maryanna Young
President, Personal Value Coaching
"Helping ordinary people achieve extraordinary dreams"
Life and Business Coach, Speaker, Author and Friend
personalvalue@aol.com
www.dontmissyourboat.com

What Brand Of Life
Are You Living?©

Tamara Schneider

A long-time friend of mine stopped by to see me, and she shared an observation about her son and his friends. She was fascinated by her six-year-old son's first experience at the carnival. What to her was a dusty, overcrowded, long line money drain, was a wonderment of lights, action, and noises to her son and his friends – a place to experience life. She laughed and asked, "How on earth was it that we could look at the same place so differently?"

I answered without hesitation, "It's your own unique Brand of Life™."

She asked, as probably many of you did - Brand of life? What does that mean? Brand is defined as a mark, characteristic, or distinctive quality. In the corporate world a brand is a unique and distinct asset of a company. We are all familiar with the various brands of clothing, shoes, and cosmetics. Likewise for people. We recognize people by the way they live – by their Brand of Life. **Brand of Life is a personal identity and lifestyle that we live consciously.**

From my experience, awareness came at a time when I doubted my professional life. By many standards, I was very successful. At the same time, I was torn by the various directions in which my life was being pulled. I needed to find a way to "live" my life in manageable pieces and focus on what was important to me. I had read enough self help books, and felt it was time to create a plan that worked for me. Through this process, I began to understand my behavior, and how I made decisions which helped me to make better choices. To live a life of my choosing became the basis for my personal Brand of Life. This knowledge equipped me to truly live my life!

Briefly stated, here are the steps that I followed. I would encourage you to follow them as well, as you work toward creating your own Brand of Life:

1. **Realize that you are already living a "Brand of Life' whether you like it or not** – This means that you are either active in making decisions for your life or you have allowed others (outside influences or environments) to make the decisions for you.

2. **Identify who you are** – Describe your behavior, passions, habits, whims, and contributions. Take a few moments and write down who you are right now. Don't use your name, address, profession, age, gender, educational credentials, marital or family status, possessions, religious affiliation or nationality. Not how others perceive you, or how you think they perceive you, but identify your very own views and values.

3. **Identify your roles** – Now you can list your age, gender, educational credentials, jobs, family status and so on. Everything you do to fulfill a job or role in your personal and professional life. These are the roles that you have actively chosen and those which you did not choose. Some examples might be a wife, husband, son, daughter, friend, writer, employee, or entrepreneur.

4. **Identify the dreamer** – You may have heard this question before, but think about it again. How would you and your life be different if money and time were not an issue? When you answer this, the unrecognized persona is brought forward. The dreamer in you is waiting to be brought into your life. And the dreamer in you is needed.

5. **Choose focal points for your life** – Look back at your lists and determine those items important for your life. Perception is our reality, so focus on points that support your ideal. Ask "Am I balanced and aligned with my values?"

6. **Act on the Focal Points** – Begin today to regularly make decisions and choose actions that will develop the habits of your personal brand. As you do this, awareness of your life increases and value-driven decisions are made. The main point here is that you are putting YOU back into your life.

7. **Have Patience with yourself** – Understand that it will take two to three weeks to develop one pattern of a decision or an action that supports your Brand of Life. You are acknowledging feelings and beliefs that may have been pushed aside for awhile. As you bring these to the forefront, these new habits will noticeably improve your quality of life. Nobody is polished on the first try, so have patience – and take the habits one or two at a time.

8. **Validate and Re-evaluate continuously** – You are living in a world that is constantly changing – so will you. It only makes sense for you to check your "barometer" and note the new and old choices for living.

9. **LIVE!** – This is the most important message of all. Of course, you will be busy with life – but in the midst of the hectic and somewhat frantic pace – don't forget to live! Which reminds me once again of my friend's son. Doesn't he embody the "living" part?

You are the sole champion of your individual, wonderful, and entire existence. The champion of

the life you lead behind a desk, in a car, in the garden, with friends or family –and- the life of your mind and imagination. This is the life of your soul. Once you understand what your brand of life means, it gives direction to your life.

So I ask – "What Brand of Life are You Living?"

– *Tamara Schneider*
CEO of Brand of Life™
Professional Speaker
info@brandoflife.com
www.brandoflife.com

My Grandfather Died Yesterday

Gloria Swardenski

I received a call yesterday from my Dad. Not an unusual event as I talk with my father often, but I could sense some heaviness in his voice as he spoke. He tried to have a few words of idle chatter, but then said, "Well, there is no easy way to put this. Your grandfather died yesterday."

My grandfather died. To some, this might be life shattering news. Those that have grown up in strong extended families might break down and sob, remembering how he used to be, and feeling the grief that comes from losing someone you love. For me, it was a little odd.

I say odd because I took a minute to try and remember my grandfather. I could barely remember his face. It had been years since I had seen him, and my memories of him are just bits and pieces of disconnected events.

I remembered being young and visiting my grandparents. We kids were not allowed to disturb the conversations of the adults, so we would often go play. Never being in the same room with him for more than a few seconds, I don't remember ever having a conversation with my grandfather in those younger years. Maybe he just didn't know what to say to a little one. But even as I grew older, he never said more than a hello to me.

When my grandfather retired, he sold his home, and he and my grandmother bought an RV so they could travel around the country. After I was married, I can remember other family members on my close-knit husband's side asking me where they were, and I never really knew. They were the gypsies who would stay in a place for just a little while and then move on when the weather would change or my grandfather decided he needed a change of scenery.

However, I do remember my grandfather making the trip from Wyoming back to Pennsylvania for my wedding. I was so amazed and excited that they were coming. Others had gotten married in the family, and they hadn't made the trip for them. I held on to some small hope that in some way I might be special. Still, even on my wedding day, he went through the reception line with everyone else, gave me a hug, and never spoke another word to me.

After years of travel, my grandparents settled in Arizona. He built a little home there in the middle of some barren place away from most everyone. I never visited him, never saw a picture, never had a call, and never got to know my grandfather.

What struck me when I received the news that my grandfather had died was not a sadness that comes from a loss of a life. It was sadness for my grandfather that he never truly learned how to live. The family had decided against doing any kind of funeral or memorial service. He had no friends. The last I heard, his children were going down to divide his things and figure out the balance of his estate. I don't know all the financial details, but I was told he had at least $100,000 in the bank.

Did my grandfather live a life of purpose? It may sound harsh to actually put it into words, but I don't think so. It is sad to think of a life just vanishing away, leaving no one to even notice. No memorial service or funeral for a man who existed on this earth for over 80 years.

So, I ask you, as I ask myself, how is your life any different? Are you living a life filled with purpose and meaning? Do you know what it means to truly live YOUR life?

If there is any one thing that I know, it is that I do not have to make the same mistakes that others in my family, including my grandfather, have made. I have the power to choose how I want to

live my life, and so do you.

When I was young, I read a Scripture passage in Jude that states, "And of some having compassion, making a difference." It was then that I made the choice to live my life in such a way that I could make a difference. That became my life's purpose.

I purposed in my heart to finish school and do so with honors, and I did. I graduated high school at 16, and immediately went to college where I graduated Valedictorian, Student Teacher of the Year, and was listed in *Who's Who Among Colleges and Universities.*

I purposed in my heart to build a home that was loving and nurturing, and I have. My husband and I have been married for 18 years now and have four beautiful children. Not any one of us is perfect, but we love one another and that makes all the difference.

And I purposed in my heart to find ways to reach out in love to others around the globe and make a difference in their lives. I am a life and business coach and have had clients from several different countries. I write a newspaper column and a daily e-zine that thousands read every day. I speak to audiences everywhere about connecting to the world around them through more effective communication skills. I own a tutoring business that supports hundreds of children and young adults every year to be more successful in school.

And there is much more I purpose yet to do!

Unlike my grandfather, when God calls me home someday, I hope to have many people come to my funeral. I would want them to come together to celebrate the end of a life that touched the hearts of many; a life that was lived with joy and compassion; a life that was truly lived with purpose.

What do you want people to say at your funeral?

– Gloria Swardenski
Life and Business Coach, Professional Speaker and Writer
Communication Expert, Author: Got 90 Seconds?
GloriaCoach@aol.com
www.gloriacoach.com

When I was growing up I always wanted to be someone. Now I realize I should have been more specific.

~ Lilly Tomlin

It Is Never Too Late To Be Who You Want To Be

YOUR PURPOSE STORY

Authors Name

Questions to Consider:

- What significant parts of your life story will impact others?

- What were the defining moments in your life that were the catalyst that helped you understand your true significance and discover your value?

_____

_____

_____

_____

_____

_____

_____

_____

_____

CO-AUTHOR BIOGRAPHIES

ELYSSE BARRETT is the President of America's Renewal, a service that provides speakers and organizations with resources to have a more effective impact. An accomplished speaker and writer, she has won essay and speech competitions and delivered speeches throughout the country. Elysse's hobbies include traveling, collecting inspirational stories, visiting with friends, and dreaming about building her own house. As the oldest of seven, Elysse's greatest love is her family. She spends much time with her family and looks forward to getting married and having a family of her own. Elysse is passionate about motivating and inspiring young people to find their purpose in Christ and learn to live up to their full potential.

DAVID BARRETT has a BA degree in mathematics and an MA degree in Family Studies. David was a leader nationally in the strong development of the Christian Education movement as a homeschool father, the leader of a homeschool organization, and since 1993, as an administrator and high school instructor at Covenant Academy, a private Christian school. David's most recent endeavor, the Biblical Worldview Learning Center, has been established to train believers in Biblical Worldview Thinking and Christian Apologetics. His passion is working with families and assisting them in living purposeful and fulfilling lives while learning to work as a team. He resides in Boise, Idaho, with his wife, Jannyce, and their seven children.

MONICA BASCIO is an Occupational Therapist and elite wheelchair athlete. After a 1992 skiing accident left her paralyzed from the waist down, she focused her efforts on her professional career and upon competing in cycling and Nordic skiing. Monica is a thirteen-time U.S. Champion and the reigning World Champion in cycling, and member of the U.S. Disabled Ski Team. She hopes to continue her skiing success at the 2006 Paralympics. Monica is also a four-time winner of the grueling Midnight Sun Ultra Challenge, a 267-mile handcycle race from Fairbanks to Anchorage, AK. In her spare time, Monica plays tennis and swims in her hometown of Evergreen, Colorado. She also sits on the Board of Directors for Colorado-based DSUSA chapter, Adaptive Adventures.

JODEE BOCK is a leadership and communication coach with One Degree in Fargo, North Dakota. One Degree makes a difference through subtle distinctions in training and development that take individuals, companies or organizations beyond their own status quo. Jodee works together with people who want to practice "riskful" thinking, as opposed to merely "wishful" thinking, by offering a safe environment to explore new ideas and discuss what really matters. They then develop a plan to transform that knowledge into action. Jodee has more than fifteen years' experience in corporate communications and organizational development.

SUZI BOYLE of Young Mortgage Service Corporation has been honored as one of the top 200 mortgage originators in the U.S. by Mortgage Originator Magazine. As the President of Young Mortgage, she is committed to excellence in her profession as well as community involvement. She sits on boards and volunteers her time for numerous community outreach organizations. Suzi speaks to various groups and individuals about positively dealing with grief following the double homicide murder of her parents. The line so many people remember Suzi frequently saying is … "I refused to remember my parents by what happened on the last day they were here on earth, but rather chose to revere them for all the unbelievable acts of love and good they contributed their sixty-eight years on this earth". Suzi lives in Boise, Idaho with her husband, Michael Hummel. Her pride and joy is her son, Jonathan who attends college in San Diego, California.

CARL DREW is a living legend in the arenas of adventure, achievement, and passion. He is a man who is achieving his dreams and inspires his audiences to achieve theirs. At the age of twenty nine, Carl is an internationally known "Hall of Fame" business award winner, international sales record breaker, adventure video producer, author, photographer, ice-climbing guide, competitive endurance athlete, and sought after inspirational speaker. Carl's presentations utilize award-winning photos and videos to weave together inspiring stories from his global adventures challenging his audiences to overcome their fears and achieve their dreams.

MARY ENZWEILER is a native and resident of the greater Cincinnati area. She has a BS degree in Pharmacy, and a Master of Education, Sports Administration degree. Mary is active on the board of the Friends of Drake Foundation, which secures philanthropic support for Drake Center, a rehabilitative hospital at which her younger brother was a patient. She has invested herself in her community as event coordinator of the Enzweiler Multi-Miler, and a board member and volunteer coordinator of the Cincinnati Flying Pig Marathon. Mary is an avid runner who now finds her passion in dedicating her life, and her running, to those who don't have the opportunity to be active. Her favorite activity is to joyously share the "little things" in life with her brother, Kent.

JOSHUA GEORGE, a two-time Paralympic bronze medalist, is a journalism major at the University of Illinois in Champaign, Illinois. He is a member of the U of I Wheelchair Basketball, Track and Road Racing teams. Joshua has competed in numerous competitions for basketball and racing across the United States, Brazil and Australia. After graduation, he will pursue a career in journalism with a focus toward magazine and newspaper writing. Joshua was a member of the USA Track and Field Team for the 2004 Paralympics in Athens.

TRAVIS S. GREENLEE is a business design and development coach who teaches people to make a more profitable living doing what they love. He specializes in working with coaches, consultants, professionals, networkers and business owners. Travis began his career with Merrill Lynch as a financial consultant and business advisor. He has been a professional trainer since 1991 and a business coach since 1994. He speaks professionally to audiences on the topics of: "The Power of Attraction", "The 21 Secrets of Master Coaches and Consultants" and "Creating Passive, Multiple Streams of Income at the Speed of Technology". Travis' passion and purpose is to make a difference in the lives of those he touches through coaching.

RICH HALLSTROM has worked as a sports broadcast specialist for 16 years, including writing, producing and performing segments that appeared on *Seahawks Saturday*. Recently, Rich co-produced the video, *A Day In The Life*. Born with a disability similar to cerebral palsy, Rich's life represents someone who has achieved greatness against all odds. As a media professional and motivational speaker, he brings unique insight into everyday challenges using his diverse life experiences. Rich is the President of Tri Strand Media and director of a non profit organization, Motivation with a Purpose. Rich counts these accomplishments as illustrations of the contribution that people with disabilities make to our society on a daily basis.

NINA HECK has been married to her husband Kim for twenty years. They have two children and two grandchildren together. Nina has a real desire to make the Bible "user-friendly" and more understandable for today's generation. Her passion to teach others about the Bible has led her to write small group Bible studies for the past ten years. Nina feels small groups are a great way to learn how the Bible is relevant in today's world. She is currently writing small group material for her church and hopes to share her life applications with other churches in the future.

KAREN HELTON never imagined that her life would have turned down the path it has taken. As a twenty-five-year old successful mother of three wonderful children, she has slowly learned to appreciate both the value in those that love her and the value in herself, which makes life just a little bit sweeter each day. Growing along with her children, Karen sees it as a unique joy to wake up every morning. However, she has decided that seeing the world through their innocent eyes is a wonderful way to view life. Karen is interested in many things, but truly passionate about music and writing, both of which she hopes to share with others for a long time to come.

DOROTHY HOBERT lives in eastern Washington. A high spirit and passion for life surround her daily. Born the oldest of six children, she is mother of three, and grandmother of four. Her treasures in life are her family and friends. Dorothy's abundance of hobbies include scrapbooking, sewing, quilting, gardening, entertaining, and traveling. A career of thirty-five years was spent in the beauty business, eight years in teaching photo journaling classes, and two years helping others find better health and financial freedom. It has been a journey full of surprises, challenges and adventures for one country girl excited about life.

DIANNE HOUGH resides in Boise, Idaho where she is a top producing realtor. Having been born and raised in Idaho (as she puts it, "locally grown" like the potatoes), Dianne has a true appreciation for the quality of life found there. Her writing exemplifies her high-energy approach to business, family and life! Dianne's positive outlook is infectious as she lives her slogan, "I'm sold on Idaho!" Dianne and lifetime husband, Bob, have two grown daughters, Angie and Kristi. Together, they enjoy hiking, biking, snow skiing and walks along the river with their Alaskan Malamute, Kodiak.

STACY JAMES is the founder and director of "Walking Victorious," a non profit organization that equips people to rise above the challenges of life. She is an inspirational speaker and author, encouraging individuals to embrace a positive attitude, courage, perseverance, and faith. Stacy is a wheelchair athlete, winning over 160 gold medals in track and field, swimming, weightlifting, and thirteen marathons. She was Ms. Wheelchair Ohio 2002 and the 2nd runner-up for Ms. Wheelchair America. Stacy served as a chaplain for the 2004 Paralympics in Athens, Greece.

FRED KNIGHT is a dentist by trade. He lives with his wife, Nadine, and their three sons in California. Fred writes for several historical societies as well as the sports page of the local newspaper. He is also known as a 'storyteller' and is happy to use his talent at various local functions. Scuba diving, falconry, photography and running a steam locomotive are just a few of the activities he enjoys with his family.

GAYE LINDFORS' business experience and engaging style bring expertise and energy to her consulting clients, keynote presentations, and workshops. With twenty-plus years as a human resources executive and business advisor and a master's degree in industrial relations, Gaye's advice has been sought by Fortune 500 companies, boards of directors, and faith-based organizations. She helps leaders create solutions by connecting the individual's desire to live a life of significance, with the organization's need to improve its organizational effectiveness. In all her work, Gaye focuses on speaking to people's hearts and minds. Gaye and her husband, Steve, live in St. Paul, Minnesota.

JEREMY NC NEWMAN has been a fiercely competitive athlete since grade school and a strength and conditioning coach since high school. In 1997 he was involved in a devastating skydiving accident and has since been confined to a wheelchair, or so it would seem. He loves to travel throughout the world sharing his story and competing as one of only two wheelchair triathlete's on the US National team. He is currently ranked #2 in the world. His mission is to share his life experiences as a keynote speaker at corporate events, business luncheons and other venues where he has the opportunity to touch, move and inspire. His passion is to deliver messages that help others overcome adversity and face challenges of their own.

RENEE' PARKER has a passion for living that she clearly reveals through written word and song. Her sphere of influence is continually expanding as she allows her inspiration of life, to pour from her soul. Creative writing is only one of the ways Renee' inspires so many. A dynamic speaker and a powerful vocalist, she has traveled abroad to share her gifts and passion with others. A native of North Carolina, Renee' works as a massage therapist and nail technician. She shares her passion and joy of life with her husband, Michael, and their three dachshunds: Jasper, Ashley and Molly.

NATALIE PETOUHOFF PhD, more commonly known as Dr. Nat, is currently a TV reporter and host reporting on gadgets, consumer technology and science. She has two television shows in development and is publishing books on inventing, goal setting and reaching your dreams. Some of her titles include: *Women Invent. They Always Have!, Get Your Invention Off The Ground, The Remote Is In Your Control™, My Life Will Be Better When…, and Infinity: That's As Far As A Girl Can GO™!* Natalie also works with people as a Life Coach, helping them overcome their own thresholds and obstacles.

KATHY PRIDE wears many hats, including author, newspaper columnist, speaker, and parent educator. Her favorite roles are as a mother to her four children, best friend to her husband, and high energy advocate for people whose hope tanks are running low. She has authored a book entitled, *H.O.P.E. For Parents: When Drugs Seduce Your Teen*. Kathy has a passion for encouraging individuals to take the worn-out tatters and loose ends of their lives and weave them into lives of new possibility. Her style is entertaining, yet transparent, as she approaches difficult topics with energy, honesty and candor. She is the director of Tapestry Ministry.

TAMARA SCHNEIDER is founder and CEO of Brand of Life - an innovative lifestyle business committed to helping you enrich your life by making positive, conscious choices. Tamara is author and publisher of the Women's Resource Guide 2003 & 2004 and is currently a Project Manager for a Fortune 10 company. She has founded and produced many innovative events included Kid's Fair – Idaho, Listener Appreciation Concerts – Idaho and Every Woman's Money Conference. She serves on a variety of boards and hosts a weekly radio segment focusing on people, places and things that enrich our lives. She is also a motivational speaker who encourages balancing personal and professional life.

SARA SEED has captivated crowds her entire life. An outstanding student-athlete, Sara was the first female to receive a collegiate athletic scholarship at Casey-Westfield High School, Casey, Illinois. As a member of the women's tennis team at Miami University, Sara was a M.A.C. conference singles champion as well as a team co-captain. In 1985 she received a B.S. in Education.

Upon graduating, she taught and coached for thirteen years at Champaign Centennial High School, Champaign, Illinois and was named "Outstanding Teacher of the Year" in 1992.

As a motivational speaker for the last sixteen years, Sara Seed has used humor, combined with her own compelling story of victory and overcoming adversity to inspire people of all ages. Now, as owner of Sara Seed Promotions, llc she continues to share her personal experiences as a businesswoman, educator, competitive athlete, and survivor of a debilitating disease with audiences across the country!

JUDY SIEGLE is one of the top elite wheelchair racers in the world. She was a member of the U.S. team in the 1996 Paralympics in Atlanta and the 2000 Paralympics in Sydney, Australia. She holds national records in four events for quadriplegic women, and was named 2000 Female Athlete of the Year by USA Wheelchair Track and Field. Judy is a Master's prepared social worker, downhill skier, and active volunteer. She travels around the United States educating, motivating, and inspiring audiences to excel in their lives. Judy is a member of the National Speakers Association.

LIZA M. SHAW MA is a Master's Level Marriage and Family Therapist and an Advanced Clinical Hypnotherapist. Since 1993, Liza has worked in many aspects of the helping profession, assisting families through traumas such as sexual abuse, domestic violence, and other types of social oppression. She has also been a practicing private psychotherapist since 1999. Liza approaches her clients with the belief that all people – no matter what their history – can overcome adversity and lead thriving lives. Liza is currently working on the publication of her first self-help book, *52 Pick-Up: The Power to Thrive, One Week at a Time.*

DOREEN BESSETTE SICOTTE was born in rural Manitoba, Canada and was educated in French and English. She is married, mother of three daughters and grandmother of eight. Before retirement, she was office manager in a collision repair shop that she co-owned. Doreen has taught classes in "A Course in Miracles," "Science of Mind" and "The Infinite Way", and considers herself a perpetual student of truth. She is an ordained minister of the International Alliance of the Churches of Truth, Canada.

MILDRED STEWART is passionate about being joyful and sharing her joy with others. Born on a farm in the early part of the century, she has seen many changes to everyday life. She now uses her eighty-seven years of life experiences as a great tool to impart wisdom to the younger generations. One of her greatest themes in life is, through the power of Christ, joy can be present day after day. Mildred currently lives in Tulsa, Oklahoma where she is active in her community. She is the mother of four, grandmother of four, and great grandmother of five.

GLORIA SWARDENSKI is an International Life and Business Coach, Syndicated Newspaper Columnist, Professional Speaker, and Owner of Gloria Jean's Tutoring. As a Master Communicator, Gloria touches lives around the globe through her unique and simple voice shared from a genuine heart.

Gloria is also the author of, *Got 90 Seconds? Quick Quotes & Notes to Encourage and Inspire* which is a powerful collection of 100 classic and contemporary quotes followed by Gloria's unique thoughts. Gloria lives in Indiana with her husband and four children who teach her how to connect to the everyday conversations in 90 seconds or less.

BRANDI SWINDELL is considered one the foremost leaders in the pro-life movement today as the co-founder and National Director of Generation Life. An active twenty-seven-year-old, she leads and organizes many pro-life projects across the nation, including successful demonstrations at the Salt Lake Olympics and the White House. Brandi has been featured nationally in: The O'Reiley Factor, The New York Times, CNN, C-Span, The Washington Post, The Washington Times, MSNBC, The Associated Press and NPR. Brandi's goal is to represent the "new face" of pro-life America. She wants others who are also young, passionate and articulate to join her in building a culture of life for the next generation. In her spare time, Brandi loves to spend time with family, hang out at Starbucks, and head to the mountains to hike in the summer and snowboard in the winter.

KATHI TUNHEIM has a spirit and energy that is both genuine and contagious allowing her to bring a fresh, exuberant approach to leadership and life. She is the President of Tunheim Leadership Group, Inc. With a thirst for learning and development, she earned her B.A. from Concordia College in Moorhead, Minn., her M.A. from the University of Wisconsin and is currently working towards a Ph.D. in Human Resources Development at the University of Minnesota in Minneapolis.

Kathi is a professional speaker who speaks in the areas of Leadership Development, Team Building and Work/Life Balance. Kathi's people-focused experience stems from an impressive career that includes over twenty years of Human Resources Development and Instructional Design. She loves life with her husband Bob and their three children, Rob, Amie and Kristie in Orono, Minnesota.

CHEE AMY VANG was born in a refugee village in Thailand after her parents swam to freedom under heavy gunfire while crossing the river that divided their home in Laos from Thailand. Earlier, they had fled to Laos from China in an attempt to gain freedom from the Communist rule over the Hmong people, from which Amy and her family are descended. The Hmong people were oppressed by the Communist Chinese government and were not allowed to become educated or advance their lives. Amy is passionate about challenging others to NOT take their life and their opportunities for granted ... especially in a country as blessed as America! Amy is a Physical Therapist Assistant and enjoys spending time with her husband and three sons.

SUSAN VITALIS MD is a medical doctor who specializes in family medicine in underserved areas around the world. Following medical school at Johns Hopkins in Baltimore, she completed a Family Medicine Residency in Minnesota and has taken her medical skills to numerous countries including Kenya, Somalia, Sudan, Rwanda, Bosnia-Herzegovina, Kosovo, Albania, Mongolia and Tibet. She loves to speak and write about her experiences and share the value and importance of taking action to respond to the needs of others, whether across the street or across the ocean. Susan splits her time between working at the Family HealthCare Center in Fargo, ND and Moorhead, MN as well as spending time with family members.

RACHAEL ZORN graduated from Wheaton College in 2002 with a B.A. in English. As the oldest daughter of former NFL quarterback Jim Zorn, she has moved throughout much of North America. Football is ranked 1st on her list of favorite sports, but after playing 4 years of college tennis it ranks a close 2nd. Adding to her adventurous life, she has worked on a political campaign, at a bank, and currently is employed by Nordstrom's corporate offices. In her spare time, Rachael cultivates her relationship with her mother, Joy, and her sisters. She also likes to run, read, talk, spend time with friends and drink coffee. Rachael currently resides in Seattle, Washington.

For more information on our Co-Authors
go to
www.dontmissyourboat.com

ABOUT THE DIRECTORS

MARYANNA YOUNG has an excitement for life that is contagious. She believes that encouragement is key for others to live out their lives with excellence. Her background includes many years as an athlete, sports coach, personal fitness trainer and event director. She developed the concept for and co-founded the Idaho Womens Fitness Celebration, one of the largest sporting events for women in the US.

Her work has taken her all over the world. She has worked with clients on national media such as ESPN, NBC, CBS, ABC and companies such as Nike, Ocean Spray, United Airlines, Asics, General Motors, Key Corp. and Bank of America. She has experience managing and coaching small business owners, entrepreneurs, non profit organizations, professional & Olympic athletes and corporate professionals.

She is President of Personal Value Coaching, and CEO of the FMG Companies where she places a high value on assisting others in taking action on their life long vision. This often means helping individuals and families merge their lifestyle and business goals.

Maryanna Young
"Helping ordinary people achieve extraordinary dreams"
Life and Business Coach, Speaker, Author and Friend
personalvalue@aol.com
www.personalvaluecoaching.com
www.dontmissyourboat.com

KIM FLETCHER is an expert in equipping individuals to discover and utilize their unique backgrounds, experiences and talents to improve every area of their lives. She loves working with individuals, small groups and large audiences in the areas of establishing vision, integrity and authenticity in the workplace, building strong personal foundations and developing leadership potential.

Her background as a college instructor and physical therapist provide her the foundation to provide significant life turnarounds for her clients. She loves speaking with young adults and professionals about developing life and career choices that are fulfilling and aligned with their values.

She is also a leading advocate worldwide for persons with disabilities. She believes that our culture is impacted as individuals affected by disability recognize their value, create new opportunities for themselves, and develop their leadership skills. She had been actively involved with Joni and Friends for over 20 years, providing disability awareness education across the nation and as far as Ghana, West Africa.

Kim is the President of Creative Life Navigation and director of Life Compass, a non profit organization.

Kim Fletcher
"Catch the Bigger Vision for Your Life"
Life Coach, Professional Speaker, Author
kimfletchercoach@aol.com
www.creativelifenavigation.com
www.dontmissyourboat.com

ACKNOWLEDGMENTS

Many thanks to:

Our Co-Authors
who have laid the foundation for thousands more
to live their lives with purpose...

Elysse Barrett
Michele Howe
Liza M Shaw
&
Gloria Swardenski
for their extraordinary editing assistance.

Nick Zelinger
at NZ Graphics for his creativity and patience
on the Cover Design and Interior Production
www.nzgraphics.com

Alison Langley
Barb Hills
at Langley Photography for the Cover Photo
www.langleyphoto.com

Angela Stewart
at
Angela R Stewart Design
for the cover concept and project prospectus
www.angelarstewartdesign.com

**Many thanks to our collective families and
friends who stood by all of us in the writing
and production process of this project.
We appreciate each of you!**

Do you long to deepen your purpose?

- Do you want your life to count for something?
- Do you long to be remembered for your positive impact on others?
- Do you currently have a passion or unique gift that is collecting dust?
- Are you attempting to live a life of significance but need motivation and encouragement?
- Do you wish to bring a greater purpose and commitment to your group or organization?

Today is the day to begin living your life with purpose

We would love to partner with you via:

Personal Coaching by phone

Live presentations to your audience

Coaching you through writing your own book or developing your own signature speaking presentation

Contact:

Kim Fletcher
Creative Life Navigation
828 327 6702

Maryanna Young
Personal Value Coaching
208 447 9036

Do You Have a Book Inside of You?

Would you like to be a Co-Author
and share your story in the next
Don't Miss Your Boat book....?

We are looking for co-authors for
***Don't Miss Your Boat:
Your Exceptional Life Begins Now***

Deadline for application:
April 30, 2005

Released – Fall 2005

For details
see
www.dontmissyourboat.com
or
contact:

Maryanna Young
at
208 344 2733

Need books....

for your family, friends or co-workers?

Copies of the Book are
available at each of
the following...

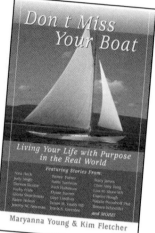

---

www.dontmissyourboat.com

Amazon.com

Websites of the Co-authors listed in this book

If you would like to order books in quantity
for your organization, company or audience,
contact:

Don't Miss Your Boat
Customer Service
208 344 2733
customerservice@dontmissyourboat.com

We want your Feedback!

The directors of *Don't Miss Your Boat* would love to hear what you think about this book!

If you have a rave review about how it has made a difference in your perspective or how it has influenced you to live your life in a more purposeful way, we would greatly appreciate hearing from you.

Don't Miss Your Boat
Product Department
1312 N 19th Street
Boise, ID 83702

or fill out the feedback form at
www.dontmissyourboat.com

Go ahead ... Live with Purpose!